239
Days

'Abdu'l-Bahá in Dublin, New Hampshire, 1912

239 Days

'Abdu'l-Bahá's Journey in America

Allan L. Ward

Bahá'í Publishing Trust / Wilmette, Illinois 60091

Library of Congress Cataloging in Publication Data

Ward, Allan L   1935—
    239 days: 'Abdu'l-Bahá's journey in America.

    Includes bibliographical references.
    1. 'Abd ul-Bahā ibn Bahā Ullāh, 1844—1921.
2. Bahaism—United States. I. Title.
BP393.W37   297'.896'30924 [B]   79-14713
ISBN 0-87743-129-9

Designed by John Solarz

Printed in the United States of America

Contents

	Illustrations	vii
	Preface	ix
1	'Abdu'l-Bahá Sails for America	3
2	First Days in America: New York City	13
3	Washington, D.C.	37
4	Chicago	47
5	Cleveland, Pittsburgh, Washington, D.C.	59
6	New York, New Jersey, Massachusetts	65
7	Magazine Accounts	77
8	New York, Philadelphia, New York	85
9	New Jersey: The Unity Feast	97
10	New York City	105
11	New Hampshire	117
12	Green Acre	125
13	Montreal	131
14	Buffalo, Chicago, Kenosha	139
15	Minnesota, Nebraska, Colorado, Utah	147
16	California	165
17	The Journey East: Teaching on the Train	173
18	The Journey East: Chicago, Cincinnati, Washington, D.C., Baltimore	177
19	Final Days in America: New York City	185
	Notes	211

Illustrations

'Abdu'l-Bahá in Dublin, New Hampshire, 1912   *Frontispiece*

Plate

I In Front of Riverside Park, New York, 1912 (above)   *between pp. 52–53*

Speaking in Plymouth Congregational Church, Chicago, May 5, 1912 (below)

II With a Group of Bahá'ís in Lincoln Park, Chicago, 1912

III Seated on a Bench in Lincoln Park, Chicago, 1912 (above)

'Abdu'l-Bahá Addressing Delegates and Friends at the Fourth Annual Bahá'í Convention on the Occasion of His Laying the Cornerstone of the Bahá'í House of Worship, Wilmette, Illinois, May 1, 1912 (below)

IV Visiting Mr. Topakyan, the Persian Consul General, Morristown, New Jersey, June 30, 1912   *between pp. 100–01*

vii

viiiIllustrations

V 'Abdu'l-Bahá at the Unity Feast, West   *between*
Englewood, New Jersey, June 29, 1912   *pp. 100–01*

VI 'Abdu'l-Bahá with a Small Group of Bahá'ís,
West Englewood, New Jersey, June 29, 1912

VII At Green Acre, Eliot, Maine, August 1912   *between*
                                                          pp. 164–65
VIII With a Group of Bahá'ís in St. Paul,
Minnesota, September 1912

IX On a Street in Kenosha, Wisconsin,
September 15, 1912 (above)

With Children on the Steps of the Home of
Helen S. Goodall, Oakland, California,
October 1912 (below)

Preface

The purpose of this book is to describe 'Abdu'l-Bahá's interaction with individuals, groups, and the press during His historic journey in America in 1912. For that growing public of every religious and philosophical background who respect and even revere 'Abdu'l-Bahá as a saintly man, a record of His daily actions encourages the development of human goodness. Many sense, as one reporter wrote, that "the divine fire of this man's spirituality is bound to illumine the dark corners of our imaginations and open up to us a spiritual realm which we would do well to go in and possess."[1] For the student and scholar of religious history, the meeting of 'Abdu'l-Bahá with the American public is a significant event, for never before during the formative years of a religion has a figure of like stature made a journey of such magnitude in a setting so different from that of His native land. For the sociologist and the psychologist and, indeed, for any discerning observer of human nature, there is much to study and ponder in the response of Western people and news media to 'Abdu'l-Bahá and in the immediate and subsequent effects of His visit on so many lives. For Bahá'ís—who believe that the Teachings of God were revealed for this age through Bahá'u'lláh and that His Son, 'Abdu'l-Bahá, demonstrated those Teachings by the example of His life—'Abdu'l-Bahá's every action, however small, concontains a lesson, an insight.

'Abdu'l-Bahá's journey to the West is an integral and compelling part of the history of the Bahá'í Faith. Its roots lie in a number of significant events: in the call of the Báb, on the night of His declaration, to the people of both East and West; in the martyrdom of the Báb and thousands of His followers for believing in the coming of the Promised One of all religions; in the forty years of exile and imprisonment suffered by that Promised One, Bahá'u'lláh, Who, in His Writings, summoned the people of the world to unity and charted the course of civilization for centuries. 'Abdu'l-Bahá, appointed by His Father as the Center of a unique Covenant with His followers, turned His attention toward the Western hemisphere and through correspondence and the dispatch of teachers raised up and nurtured a body of followers. Although some of them made pilgrimages, beginning in 1898, to the Holy Land to meet Him, the majority were obliged to await His journey in 1912 before they could be in His presence; hear His words, directions, and admonitions; and see the living example of Bahá'u'lláh's Teachings. 'Abdu'l-Bahá prepared this growing group of believers to receive, a few years later, a document entitled *Tablets of the Divine Plan*, in which he requested them to take the new Revelation to all the people of the world.

'Abdu'l-Bahá's earthly mission ended in 1921. During the following sixteen years Shoghi Effendi, the grandson whom 'Abdu'l-Bahá appointed Guardian of the Faith, labored to build up the administrative order of the Bahá'í Faith as a necessary requisite for its worldwide expansion. In 1937 he launched a series of plans to implement

'Abdu'l-Bahá's directives in a systematic fashion. Today
The Universal House of Justice, the central authority of
the Bahá'í Faith, continues to carry out 'Abdu'l-Bahá's
Plan through a series of global plans, leading toward the
establishment of a spiritually ordered world, and, as
Bahá'ís believe, the Kingdom of God on earth.
'Abdu'l-Bahá's journey, then, stands as a link between the
martyrdom, exile, and revelations of two Manifestations
of God, and the spread of Bahá'u'lláh's Teachings
throughout the planet.

For further detail about the early Western Bahá'ís
whose names intertwine with the events related to
'Abdu'l-Bahá the reader can refer to biographies about
them and to the increasing number of essays and articles
being published, most notably in *Bahá'í News*, *World
Order*, and the volumes of *The Bahá'í World*. Such information is not included here, since my purpose is not to record
the backgrounds and accomplishments of those first
American Bahá'ís but to focus on 'Abdu'l-Bahá's interaction with and impact on them.

In gathering historical information about 'Abd-
u'l-Bahá's journey in America, notes, diaries, and news
accounts are vital and valuable resources. But just as a
reflection of something in a mirror is limited by the properties of the reflective surface, each individual's reflection
of events relating to 'Abdu'l-Bahá was influenced by personal understanding, attitudes, and values. For example,
in reading the words a reporter attributed to 'Abdu'l-Bahá,
we must keep in mind that the account may be an accu-
rate rendering of what the reporter remembered
'Abdu'l-Bahá's saying but, in fact, may not be the exact
words of or have the precise emphasis intended by
'Abdu'l-Bahá; moreover, through carelessness or prej-

udice, the news story may be completely misleading or inaccurate. In addition, we must be aware that 'Abdu'l-Bahá generally spoke in Persian, which a translator rendered immediately into English; the translator may not always have chosen words that gave 'Abdu'l-Bahá's exact meaning. We must also remember that personal accounts and diaries are just that—an individual's notes that may or may not reflect accurately what 'Abdu'l-Bahá said or did. Yet despite the myriad possibilities of seeing Perfection imperfectly reflected in an account utilizing such sources, we can sense the impact 'Abdu'l-Bahá had on believer and unbeliever alike and gain a better understanding of the Perfect Exemplar. However, without exception, for 'Abdu'l-Bahá's exact Teachings we should consult His own authorized and published Writings rather than words attributed to Him by others.

Any book of this scope is ultimately a group effort, and full acknowledgment is impossible. Those individuals and representatives of Local Spiritual Assemblies across the country who traced magazine and newspaper articles and sent them to the Publishing Trust contributed not only to this publication but to the building in the National Bahá'í Archives of a lasting legacy for future historians. To the National Bahá'í Archives itself I am grateful for access to photographs of 'Abdu'l-Bahá.

As we follow the journey of 'Abdu'l-Bahá across a continent, we can recall the words He spoke to those who surrounded Him at his first meeting in America: "This long voyage will prove how great is my love for you."[2] That love is with us still.

ALLAN L. WARD

239 Days

1

'Abdu'l-Bahá Sails for America

'Abdu'l-Bahá was in America for 239 days, from April 11 until December 5, in the year 1912.* For two decades prior to that time there had been Bahá'í activities in the United States and Canada. The first public mention of the Bahá'í Faith in America was in a talk prepared by the Reverend Henry H. Jessup and delivered, in his absence, by another reader to the World Parliament of Religions in Chicago in 1893.[1] The first American to become a follower of Bahá'u'lláh was Thornton Chase. Within a few years there were groups in several American cities.

One of the persons who had read of Jessup's presentation was Mrs. Lua Getsinger, who became a Bahá'í and introduced the Faith to Mrs. Phoebe Hearst. Mrs. Hearst was influential in organizing, in 1898, the first group of Bahá'ís to travel by boat to the Holy Land—the first Western

---

*'Abdu'l-Bahá is a title, in Arabic, meaning "The Servant of the Glory [of God]." Since many of the references in this volume were written before orientalists systematized the transliteration of Persian and Arabic words, many variations in spelling appear. 'Abdu'l-Bahá's given name is 'Abbás; "Effendi" is a title roughly equivalent to "Mr." in English. Reporters used different combinations of 'Abdu'l-Bahá's given name and His titles, so that He is referred to variously as "'Abbás Effendi," "'Abdu'l-Bahá 'Abbás," and so on.

Bahá'ís to meet 'Abdu'l-Bahá. The pilgrims returned and taught the Faith, until there were groups across the United States and in several locations in Canada and Europe.

In 1908 the Young Turks Revolution took place, overthrowing 'Abdu'l-Ḥamíd's government and freeing religious prisoners, including 'Abdu'l-Bahá. Thus ended the years of imprisonment and detainment that began when the Persian government exiled His Father Bahá'u'lláh from Ṭihrán, by stages, to the Turkish penal colony of 'Akká. The Bahá'í Faith, which the Turkish and Persian authorities had hoped to exterminate by banishing its Founder and Head to a remote prison city, not only had refused to be exterminated but by 1908 had begun to spread from the East to the West. The early believers in America, when they learned of 'Abdu'l-Bahá's freedom, began requesting Him to visit the United States. He explained in various ways that it was not possible at the time, that He could not come until there was greater unity among the American friends. The inquiries continued, and He stated emphatically:

> . . . In view of the differences among the friends and the lack of unity . . . how can Abdul-Baha hasten to those parts? . . .
>
> If the friends . . . long for the visit of Abdul-Baha they must immediately remove from their midst differences of opinion and be engaged in the practice of infinite love and unity. . . . Under such a condition, how can they arise to guide the people of the world and establish union and harmony between the nations of the earth? . . .
>
> Verily, verily, I say unto you, were it not for this difference amongst you, the inhabitants of America in

all those regions would have, by now, been attracted to the Kingdom of God, and would have constituted themselves your helpers and assisters. . . .

I beg of God to confirm you in union and concord that you may become the cause of the oneness of the kingdom of humanity.[2]

The general public first heard of 'Abdu'l-Bahá through books and through magazine and newspaper articles. As early as 1892 the Cambridge University orientalist, Professor E. G. Browne, had visited the Holy Land and had written, in addition to his much-quoted description of Bahá'u'lláh, the first description by a Westerner of 'Abdu'l-Bahá, in his introduction to A Traveller's Narrative:

Seldom have I seen one whose appearance impressed me more. A tall strongly-built man holding himself straight as an arrow, with white turban and raiment, long black locks reaching almost to the shoulder, broad powerful forehead . . . eyes keen as a hawk's, and strongly-marked but pleasing features—such was my first impression of 'Abbás Efendí. . . . Subsequent conversation with him served only to heighten the respect with which his appearance had from the first inspired me. One more eloquent of speech, more ready of argument, more apt of illustration, more intimately acquainted with the sacred books of the Jews, the Christians, and the Muhammadans, could, I should think, scarcely be found. . . . These qualities, combined with a bearing at once majestic and genial, made me cease to wonder at the influence and esteem which he enjoyed even beyond the circle of his father's followers. About the greatness of this man and his power no one who had seen him could entertain a doubt.[3]

A reporter, Ethel Stefana Stevens, went to the Holy Land and stayed with 'Abdu'l-Bahá and His family for several months. In 1911 her account was printed in *Everybody's Magazine* under the title "The Light in the Lantern." The editor's forenote to the article stated, *"For seventy years a religion without church, priest, creed, or fixed form of worship has been spreading through the Orient, claiming converts and martyrs by thousands. . . . This movement . . . has also extended to Europe, Great Britain, Hawaii, and the United States. . . ."* In the twelve-page article, Miss Stevens noted about 'Abdu'l-Bahá:

This servant of Baha is a man with shrewd, kindly, courteous eyes that seem to look into you instead of at you, but that instinctively make you like them and all that goes with them. . . .

Regard him well, my friends, for in him you behold one of the most significant figures in the religious world to-day; . . .

. . . He possesses to a positively miraculous degree the faculty of interesting himself in every human soul that asks his spiritual or material aid. . . . But above all, he possesses that subtler quality of spirituality which is felt rather than understood by those with whom he comes in contact. Gentle, genial, and courteous always, he receives, instructs, advises, and assists with unfailing tact and understanding the cosmopolitan stream of pilgrims which flows so steadily and so increasingly toward this little Syrian coast town. . . .

The Effendi himself . . . lives in the utmost simplic-

ity. His own bedroom is almost Spartan in its plainness.
A bowl of soup and a dish of rice usually compose his
heartiest meal. . . .

. . . The Effendi is a keen and clever controversialist;
his verbal parries and thrusts are quick as rapier-
strokes, as has been learned to their discomfiture by
theologians of all creeds who have visited Haifa for the
sole purpose of confuting him with their arguments. So
highly is he respected, even among the most bigoted
followers of Islam, that many Moslem ecclesiastics of
note have stopped at Haifa to pay him a visit of ceremony on their way to the Holy Cities.

Nor does he confine himself to things spiritual and
theoretical. He takes a lively interest in those political,
social, and educational movements of the Western
world. . . .

And this versatility, this capacity to reason and form
suggestive theories on any subject, is all the more amaz-
ing when one remembers that Abbas Effendi, exiled to
Bagdad with his father before he was six, and for forty
years a jealously guarded prisoner at Acre, where he
was wholly cut off from the world of culture, has never
known a single year of schooling. . . .

. . . he is a sincere, courageous man, a figure whose
increasing influence is already world-wide in its
significance.[4]

When 'Abdu'l-Bahá first left Haifa in 1910, He did not
generally inform the friends. Sydney Sprague, visiting
the Holy Land at that time, wrote Mrs. Isabella Britting-
ham:

I have a very big piece of news to tell you. Abdul-

Baha has left this Holy Spot for the first time in forty-two years, and has gone to Egypt. . . . Everyone was astounded to hear of Abdul-Baha's departure, for no one knew. . . . The afternoon of the day he left, he came to . . . see us and sat with us a while. . . . That night, as usual, the believers gathered before the house of Abdul-Baha to receive that blessing, which every day is ours, of being in his presence, but we waited in vain, for one of the sons-in-law came and told us that Abdul-Baha had taken the Khedivial steamer for Port Said. . . . after forty-two years in this cage, the Divine Bird has spread His wings and in perfect freedom flown away.[5]

'Abdu'l-Bahá remained in Africa until 1911, when He made His first historic visit to Europe; then He returned to Africa, where He remained until the spring of the next year. Maḥmúd-i Zarqání, who traveled with Him as His secretary and who kept a diary, wrote:

Leaving Ramlih on the morning of Monday, . . . (March 25, 1912) His Holiness bade adieu to friends and to the Leaves of the Blessed Tree. . . .*
At the time of leave taking, He embraced and permitted all the friends to go, yet they followed Him to the steamer. Each heart, full of sighs and sorrows, was dejected on account of the separation from the Manifest Beauty.† After a little talk in the steamer about the

---

*"Leaves" refers to the women in the household of Bahá'u'lláh and 'Abdu'l-Bahá.
†One of the many titles used in referring to 'Abdu'l-Bahá.

allotment of cabins, His Holiness seated Himself in the salon and began to console and comfort the friends and relatives for an hour before departure. The S.S. *Cedric* of White Star Line became the bearer of the Most Holy Temple . . . and with great majesty and pride, it steamed out of Alexandria.

There were six persons with His Holiness, namely, His Holiness Shoghi Effendi, Siyyid Assadu'lláh, Dr. Faríd, Mírzá Munír, Áqá <u>Kh</u>osrow, and the writer, Áqá Mírzá Maḥmúd-i Zarqání.[6]

The American friends had sent thousands of dollars for 'Abdu'l-Bahá's journey, urging Him to leave the *Cedric* in Italy, as many of the passengers were doing, to travel by rail and boat to England, and there to sail on the maiden voyage of the *Titanic*. 'Abdu'l-Bahá returned the money for charity and continued His voyage to America on the *Cedric*.

When the ship stopped at Naples, Maḥmúd wrote, on March 29:

Some of the American friends, who were waiting for the steamer, came to see the Beloved. Mr. and Mrs. Woodcock of Canada, Mr. and Mrs. Austin of Denver and Miss Mathew of London accompanied Him to New York. The talk of the day was that a party of doctors was to board the steamer at Naples to examine the eyes of the passengers. The doctor on ship board had already given his opinion about the affection in Áqá <u>Kh</u>osrow's eyes. When these doctors came and examined the eyes of the passengers, they declared the eyes of Áqá Shoghi Effendi and Mírzá Munír were also affected and

that they should return. The doctors persisted that even
if they went to New York, they should have to return.
The Beloved, therefore, ordered them to obey.

On March 30, Mahmúd continued:

The Beloved bestowed utmost favors, kindness and
blessings on the three and bade them farewell. They left
the steamer deeply affected and in great dejec-
tion. . . . The Beloved said, "There is a wisdom in this
matter which will become known later." The day was
spent when the steamer left Naples direct for New York.
Henceforth there were with the Beloved three
Persians—Áqá Siyyid Assadu'lláh, Dr. Faríd and this
servant (Áqá Mírzá Mahmúd) and six western
friends—Mr. and Mrs. Woodcock, Miss Woodcock,
Mr. and Mrs. Austin and Miss Mathew, who, with
great joy and happiness, enjoyed the Blessed Presence.

As the ship passed the Rock of Gibraltar on April 3,
'Abdu'l-Bahá surveyed the area with field glasses and
spoke of the conquests of the Muhammadans. As he paced
back and forth on deck, He said, "'Up to the present time
no one has traveled from Persia to America in this manner.
Some have gone, but for their personal gain and for tri-
fling things. It may be said that it is the first voyage of the
Easterners to America. I have strong hopes of divine
assistance—so that He will open the doors of victory and
conquest on all sides. Today, all the nations of the world
are vanquished and victory and glory revolve around the
servants of the Blessed Perfection [Bahá'u'lláh]. All aims
must be set aside except this one grand aim. Hardships
and disgrace in this path are, therefore, comforts and

honor, and the persecution of the soul, is a blessing.'"

'Abdu'l-Bahá thus made it clear that He did not set His course toward America to seek His own glory or to spread His own message. He said, when He reached His destination, that it was His "'purpose to set forth in America the fundamental principles of the revelation and teachings of Baha 'Ullah. It will then become the duty of the Bahais . . . to give these principles unfoldment and application in the minds, hearts and lives of the people.'"[7] 'Abdu'l-Bahá's name means the Servant of the Glory, and He came to America in that capacity—the Servant of Bahá'u'lláh, appointed by His Father as the Center of His Covenant and the Perfect Exemplar of the Faith of Bahá'u'lláh. He came to reinforce the efforts of those few early believers in America and to give them a living Example of what it means to be a Bahá'í. In short, He came to unify and to deepen those early believers and to teach them the significance of firmness in the Covenant that Bahá'u'lláh had made with the Bahá'ís. He came to set in motion teaching efforts, the effects of which would be felt around the world. He came to sow seeds that would germinate, sprout, grow, and bear fruit for a millenium —that, in fact, would hasten the advent of the millenium.

The effects of the presence of 'Abdu'l-Bahá were such that by the end of the voyage from Africa, many people were seeking His presence and asking for His address in New York. At 9:00 P.M. on April 10, as the lights of the city glimmered in the distance, the ship anchored, ready to enter the New York harbor the next morning.

2

First Days in America:
New York City

The next day was Thursday, April 11, 1912, 'Abdu'l-Bahá's first day in America. As the *Cedric* came up the bay, reporters went out on the tugboat to board the ship at quarantine in order to interview 'Abdu'l-Bahá. Among them was Wendell Phillips Dodge, of the New York City News Association, whose report was sent out through the Associated Press. He wrote:

When the ship news reporters boarded the *Cedric* down the bay Abdul-Baha was found on the upper deck, standing where he could see the pilot, his long, flowing oriental robe flapping in the breeze. . . .

His face was light itself as he scanned the harbor and greeted the reporters. . . .

His first words were about the press, saying:

"The pages of swiftly appearing newspapers are indeed the mirror of the world. . . . But it behooveth the editors of the newspapers to be sanctified from the prejudice of egotism and desire, and to be adorned with the ornament of equity and justice."

When the ship was abreast the Statue of Liberty, standing erect and facing it, Abdul-Baha held his arms wide apart in salutation, and said:

"There is the new world's symbol of liberty and freedom. After being forty years a prisoner I can tell you that freedom is not a matter of place. It is a condition. Unless one accept dire vicissitudes he will not attain. When one is released from the prison of self, that is indeed a release.". . .

The ship now pointed its nose up the North River, and gazing . . . at the . . . skyscrapers, [He said]:

"These are the minarets of Western World commerce and industry. . . ."

The ship now reached its pier, where were anxiously waiting several hundred Baha'is . . . who had been craning their necks down the river for a first sight of him since early morning.[1]

The passengers disembarked, but 'Abdu'l-Bahá remained on board and called for Edward B. (Saffa) Kinney to come to Him.[2] Mr. Kinney returned with 'Abdu'l-Bahá's wish that the Bahá'ís disperse and His promise to meet them at the Kinney home that afternoon.

Some of the Bahá'ís, however, were undaunted. Juliet Thompson, in her diary that day noted that she, Rhoda Nichols, and Marjorie Morton decided they would not leave until they had seen Him. So they flattened themselves against a recessed window below the pier entrance, Rhoda Nichols still clutching a long box of lilies she had brought. Just then the driver of Mountfort Mills' car drove it forward, parking directly in front of them, and 'Abdu'l-Bahá walked through the pier entrance with Howard MacNutt and Mills toward the car. Juliet Thompson wrote, "In a panic we waited. . . . As the Master was stepping into the car, He turned and—*smiled* at us."

From the pier, 'Abdu'l-Bahá drove to the Hotel Ansonia, went to His suite (which had two bedrooms, a small drawing room, kitchen, and bath), and took a cup of tea. Then He drove to West End Avenue to the Kinney home where several hundred people awaited Him. He greeted them saying, "How are you? Welcome! Welcome! After arriving today, although weary with travel, I had the utmost longing and yearning to see you and could not resist this meeting. Now that I have met you, all my weariness has vanished, for your meeting is the cause of spiritual happiness."[3] After He spoke, He talked to each person individually. As He left, they followed Him from the house and crowded around His carriage until He left for the hotel.

On April 11 and 12, the newspapers chronicled His arrival with varying degrees of accuracy:

New York City Sun: "PROPHET OF BAHAIS HERE. . . .

". . . Arthur Pillsbury Dodge, a lawyer, who imported the belief, said . . . that there were probably 20,000,000 Bahais in the world and that the belief was gaining ground rapidly."

New York City Evening Mail: "BANISHED FIFTY YEARS, LEADER OF BAHAI HERE: PERSIAN PHILOSOPHER FAVORS WOMAN SUFFRAGE AND WILL TALK PEACE. . . .

"Abdul Baha was greeted by fully a thousand of his followers in America, principally New Yorkers."

New York Evening World: "ABDUL BAHA ABBAS IS HERE TO PREACH BROTHERLY LOVE. . . .

"Abbas Effendi was met at the pier by a party of about forty prosperous looking persons. . . ."

New York City Evening World: "PERSIAN TEACHER

OF WORLD-PEACE IS HERE

"'Khosohamadid.'

"This is Persian, meaning 'Howdy' or 'Welcome.' It was spoken by Abdul Baha Abbas. . . .

". . . He said:

"'I have two reasons in coming to this country. The first is to travel and see your places of interest . . . as any ordinary tourist might do. I do not come to make converts to the Bahai movement. . . .'

"Abdul Baha Abbas will remain in America four months and then go to Japan and China."

New York Herald: "ABDUL BAHA HERE TO CONVERT AMERICA TO HIS PEACE DOCTRINE

"Abdul Baha will begin his work of converting America at the Peace Conference at Lake Mohonk late this month, and thereafter will be heard at colleges, churches and gatherings of earnest persons throughout the land.

"Abdul Baha's philosophy is of a sort which the Occidental mind does not grasp in the first sentence. . . ."

New York City Sun: "DISCIPLES HERE HAIL ABDUL BAHA

". . . [He] was welcomed reverently by more than three hundred of his American disciples yesterday. . . . Catholics, Protestants, Jews and Mohammedans joined in the reception. . . ."

New York City World: "PERSIAN TEACHER OF WORLD PEACE ARRIVES. . . .

"Abdul is sixty-eight, but looks ninety. . . . His voice is strong."

Associated Press release: "He is strongly and solidly built. . . . he appeared alert and active in every movement, his head thrown back and splendidly poised upon his broad, square shoulders. . . . a large, massive head, full-domed and remarkably wide across the forehead and temples, the forehead rising like a great palisade above the eyes, which were very wide apart, their orbits large and deep. . . ."[4]

New York Times: "ABDUL BAHA HERE.

". . . he and his father, Ben Ullah [Bahá'u'lláh] . . . were exiled by the Turkish Government fifty years ago.

"Abdul Baha comes to us on a mission of peace and will deliver one of his principle addresses before the Peace Conference at Lake Mohonk. . . ."

New York City Evening World: "ABDUL BAHA ABBAS, HEAD OF NEWEST RELIGION, BE-LIEVES IN WOMAN SUFFRAGE AND DIVORCE.

". . . members of the sect were known originally as Babists, after The Bab, but they are now called Bahais, after the Bahas, father and son. . . .

"Of course nobody could be named Baha without having a beard. . . .

"He has brought a suite of five very Oriental gentlemen. . . .

"Abdul Baha is really a delightful prophet. He says he isn't a prophet, by the way, but 'only a servant of the servants of God.' . . .

"The prophet wore . . . A modern looking gray over-coat, with a plaid lining, half concealing a gown of snuff-colored cloth that was knotted with a cord about the middle like a bath robe. . . .

". . . I ventured an interruption.

"'But you see there is another remedy for strife among religions,' I said to the interpreter, 'and New York seems to have found it. Tell the prophet that we are really a lot of heathens and that we don't need to kiss and make up—we need to believe—what has he for us to believe?'

"The doctor interpreter eyed me and I was very glad that I wasn't in Persia. . . ."

New York City Evening Sun: "AN APOSTLE OF PEACE. . . . The keynote of Abdul Baha's philosophy is that men serve God best by serving their kind. . . ."

The next day Leo Slezak made his seasonal farewell appearance in opera and Toscanini, his last appearance until fall. It was Friday, April 12, 'Abdu'l-Bahá's second day in America.

From early morning people were lined up at His hotel suite to meet Him. Each interview was a precious gem, set for the needs of the individual. Many could echo the words of the Unitarian minister, Howard Colby Ives, who concluded his account of his meeting with 'Abdu'l-Bahá that morning by writing, "life has never been quite the same since."[5] Telephone calls came continually with requests for interviews and invitations to speak to various groups.

That afternoon 'Abdu'l-Bahá said to a thousand persons in the MacNutt home, "Array yourselves in the perfection of divine virtues. I hope you may be quickened and vivified by the breaths of the Holy Spirit. Then shall ye indeed become the angels of heaven whom Christ promised would appear in this Day to gather the harvest of divine planting. This is my hope. This is my prayer for you."[6]

Later that same Friday He spoke to another thousand people in Miss Phillips' studio, saying, "Do you appreciate the Day in which you live?" and telling them, "Strive with all the power of your souls, your deeds, actions and words to assist the spread of these glad-tidings. . . ."[7]

The *New York Herald*, the next day, spoke of 'Abdu'l-Bahá's "speedy tour of busy New York," in an article headed, "ABDUL BAHA, DAZED BY CITY'S RUSH, CALLS NEW YORK A BEEHIVE:"

> Abdul Baha Abbas, promotor of the new religious code . . . crossed the Williamsburg Bridge and went to the home of Howard MacNutt . . . thence to the houses of a few friends, to the Cooper Institute and back across the Williamsburg Bridge through the east side at the rush hour. Then he visited homes of friends and went back for a brief rest in his luxurious apartment in the Ansonia. And how he did relish that cup of coffee—Turkish coffee—as he sat down in a red plush chair. . . . Abdul Baha has his cloak lined with sable fur, and he loves children—and Turkish delight, which species of candy decorated a table in one of the rooms of the large apartment. It was said that Abdul Baha had brought the Turkish delight all the way from the land where he had been imprisoned for many years.

On Saturday, April 13, the newspapers reported that Clara Barton, the founder of the Red Cross had died, and that Enrico Caruso had sung his last show of the season. The *New York City Evening Mail* editorial page commented on 'Abdu'l-Bahá:

> Don't laugh at Abdul Abbas. He has an idea. . . . people with ideas generally are laughed at. But after the world has laughed long enough, it turns around and eats

the idea very solemnly and very greedily, and digests it, and makes it part of its bone and fiber.

Abdul's idea is that all religions are actually the same, and absolutely one. . . .

A side idea of Abdul's is that things modern are just as good as things ancient. This notion makes the white-bearded and snowy-turbaned leader exactly as much at home on Broadway as he was in the lonely cell at Acre. . . .

We are not personally acquainted with Abdul Abbas, and we cannot tell how much of charlatanry may be mixed up with his doctrine. But the idea in itself is good stuff. Another religious teacher, who had some points of resemblance to Abdul, once went so far as to say that there is "neither Jew nor Greek, nor bond nor free, nor male nor female." . . . he is the strange anomaly of an oriental mystic who believes in woman suffrage and in Broadway. He is worth his picture in the papers.

'Abdu'l-Bahá met that day with an endless flow of visitors, including a group of ministers. After talking to them, He received the Reverend J. T. Bixby, who came to interview Him for an article for the *North American Review*. When Bixby asked Him if *A Traveller's Narrative* was "substantially correct," not knowing that 'Abdu'l-Bahá had authored it, He answered, "It is an authority." When Bixby questioned some of Browne's writings, 'Abdu'l-Bahá said Browne "interviewed various people and automatically wrote down all he heard. Naturally when he met enemies of Baha'o'llah he heard nothing favorable. Would you go to the Vatican to hear praises of the Protestants? Would you consult Jewish rabbis as to the reality of Christ?" To Bixby's questions concerning prayer, 'Abdu'l-Bahá replied, "It matters not whether we bend the head in the East or the knee in the West. The purpose of prayer is to come nearer to God. . . ." He explained at length progressive revelation and the relationship of the Manifestations; and, when the interview ended, He laid an enormous bunch of white roses in Bixby's arms.[8]

When He spoke to an immense crowd at Mrs. Marjorie Morton's home that afternoon, He stood on the staircase, His translator standing a step below Him. When the translator could not render *tábistán* into English, after a dead silence, 'Abdu'l-Bahá laughed and said to him, "Summer!"[9]

The newspapers for Sunday, April 14, told of citizens of the United States fleeing Mexico and General Orozco's repudiation of the U. S. Consul; had advertisements for the musical *Kismet*, starring Otis Skinner, and for the "positively last week" of the Barnum and Bailey Circus at Madison Square Garden; noted that J. P. Morgan was to celebrate his seventy-fifth birthday that week; and indicated that the *Titanic* was due to arrive on Wednesday.

On His first Sunday in America 'Abdu'l-Bahá spoke at the Church of the Ascension, located at Fifth Avenue and Tenth Street. Dr. Percy Stickney Grant, the minister, had, just a few months before, warned his congregation about the "Baha'i sect," and made "thundering denunciations of . . . the slumbering and superstitious Orient— the Orient that brought to the West 'nothing but disease and death.' . . ." But in March 1912 he wrote Juliet Thompson, a long-time acquaintance, saying, ". . . I shall be more than happy to invite him to the Ascension pulpit

in my place. I should like to show so important and
splendid a person, and those who love him, whatever
hospitality and goodwill can be expressed. . . ."[10]

'Abdu'l-Bahá arrived at the rectory at 10:30 A.M. The
New York Herald noted that the "Announcement that
Abdul Baha would make an address, drew so great a
throng to the church that every seat was filled and many
sat on the steps of the chancel." 'Abdu'l-Bahá waited in the
vestry-room as the service began. The processional
marched in, with Juliet Thompson, the Persian friends,
and Edward Getsinger completing it. The altar and chancel were banked with calla lilies. As the choir sang "Jesus
Lives," 'Abdu'l-Bahá entered hand in hand with Dr.
Grant, who led Him to the Bishop's chair and introduced
Him to the congregation of two thousand, saying, "'It is a
personal gratification that I have the honor and pleasure to
welcome to this place of worship a messenger from the
East, freshly bearing a message of the gospel of peace,
good will and love to all mankind. In him we see a master
of the things of the spirit.'"[11]

'Abdu'l-Bahá began, "In his scriptural lesson this morning the revered Doctor read a verse from the Epistle of St.
Paul to the Corinthians, 'For now we see through a glass
darkly, but then face to face.' The light of truth has
heretofore been seen dimly through variegated glasses,
but now the splendors of divinity shall be visible through
the translucent mirrors of pure hearts and spirits." After
His talk, 'Abdu'l-Bahá raised His hands, palms upward,
and prayed, "O Almighty! O God! O Thou compassion-
ate One! This servant of thine has hastened to the regions
of the west from the uttermost parts of the east that
perchance these nostrils may be perfumed by the fra-

grances of thy bestowals; that the breeze of the rose-
garden of guidance may blow over these cities. . . ."[12]
"Christ Our Lord Has Risen Again," the recessional
hymn, began; and when 'Abdu'l-Bahá left the Church, the
people flocked about Him.

On Monday morning the *New York Herald* reported,
"ABDUL BAHA IN EPISCOPAL PULPIT Leader of
Oriental Cult Causes Stir by Preaching in Church of the
Ascension." The article continued:

> Some of the congregation . . . and members of other
> Episcopal churches expressed astonishment that a re-
> ligious leader not professing Christianity should have
> been invited to preach and permitted to offer prayer
> within the chancel at a regular Episcopal service. . . .
> It was said that Canon Nineteen of the Episcopal
> Church forbids any one not episcopally ordained from
> preaching in an Episcopal pulpit without the consent of
> the bishop. There is no provision against a non-
> ordained person offering prayer within the chancel, it
> was said, because no such contingency was anticipated.

After an exchange of opinions in the paper by various
persons of the church the Bishop himself came to
'Abdu'l-Bahá and thanked Him for coming to the church.
'Abdu'l-Bahá spoke with him about the injuriousness of
dogmas and imitations.

The ceaseless flow of visitors to see 'Abdu'l-Bahá produced interesting combinations of visitors. Among the
Monday crowds were an inventor of arms and explosives
and the secretary of the New York Peace Society. Mr. W.
H. Short, of the Peace Society, was the first to greet

'Abdu'l-Bahá, saying, "'All the members of the New York Peace Society feel the truth and inspiration of what you have said.'"

When Mr. Hudson Maxim, the munitions manufacturer, entered, the dialogue took a different turn:

Abdul-Baha. "Welcome! Welcome! Very welcome!"

Hudson Maxim. "I am glad to hear you speak English."

A.B. "My life has been spent in the Orient where foreign languages are seldom used. Otherwise I would have acquired English. . . ."

H.M. "Are you speaking in Turkish?"

A.B. "In Persian. I also speak Turkish and Arabic; Turkish is very difficult. . . ."

H.M. "I understand that you are a messenger of peace to this country. What is your opinion about modern war? . . ."

A.B. "Everything that prevents war is good."

H.M. "Christ said He came to make war. . . ."

A.B. "We have the history of the world for nearly six thousand years. . . . Let us now try peace for a while. If good results follow, let us adhere to it. If not let us throw it away and fight again. Nothing will be lost by the experiment." . . .

H.M. "Do you consider the next great national war necessary?"

A.B. "I hope your efforts may be able to prevent it. . . ."

. . . .

H.M. "Fewer are killed in modern engagements than in the battles of ancient times; the range is longer and the action less deadly."

A.B. "How about the war between Japan and Russia?"

H.M. "Less men are killed in war in a year now than are killed by our industries through preventable accidents."

A.B. "War is the most preventable accident."

H.M. [Making diagram.] "The effect of a bomb is not so great as expected. . . . If its explosive energy could be expended in the right direction, it would do plenty of killing."

. . . .

A.B. "You are a celebrated inventor and scientific expert whose energies and faculties are employed in the production of means for human destruction. Your name has become famous in the science of war. Now you have the opportunity of becoming doubly famous. You must practice the science of peace. . . . invent guns of love which shall shake the foundations of humanity. . . .

". . . Then it will be said by the people of the world, this is Mr. Maxim, inventor of the guns of war, discoverer of high explosives, military scientist, who has also discovered and invented means for increasing the life and love of man; who has put an end to the strife of nations and uprooted the tree of war. . . . Then will your name be recorded in the pages of history with a pen of gold. . . ."[13]

On Tuesday, April 16, the *New York Times* headline read, "TITANIC SINKS FOUR HOURS AFTER HITTING ICEBERG."

As the crowds kept coming to see 'Abdu'l-Bahá, Maḥmúd noted, "The friends and inquirers continued coming successively from early in the morning to late in the afternoon. There was always a group sitting outside waiting for its turn. If they were granted a private interview by Him of only five minutes, they considered themselves greatly favored." Juliet Thompson wrote on that same day, "Later, May Maxwell and I were together in the Master's room. He was lying back on His pillow, May's baby crawling over Him, feeding first the baby, then May and me with chocolates."

On Wednesday, April 17, the day that Miss Quimby became the first woman pilot to fly across the English channel in an "aeroplane," a number of ministers came to request 'Abdu'l-Bahá to speak in their churches; but He explained that He was leaving soon for Chicago. In addition, He had other matters of great importance to attend to. Mahmúd, in recording 'Abdu'l-Bahá's concern for racism, the most challenging issue in American society, wrote:

> As there existed enmity between the white and the colored races in America to such a degree that the white did not allow the colored to attend their meetings and other public functions, the Beloved strongly urged the friends to associate with each other in utmost joy and happiness. A successful meeting was convened in the home of Mr. Kinney where the audience consisted of friends and outsiders of both races—white and colored.

'Abdu'l-Bahá, the Exemplar, served these friends a meal which He prepared Himself, at the home of Mr. and Mrs. Edward B. Kinney. "It was," Mahmúd wrote, "a magnificent supper." 'Abdu'l-Bahá told the friends, among other things, "Become as waves of one sea, trees of one forest, growing in the utmost love, agreement and unity."[14]

On Thursday, April 18, Marconi made his first public appearance in America. 'Abdu'l-Bahá went to a Broadway play that afternoon, *The Terrible Meek*, which dealt with the crucifixion of Christ. He returned from the play to the hotel where the crowds were waiting. Among the visitors was Kate Carew, the reporter for the *New York Tribune* whose caustic style mellowed in the presence of 'Abdu'l-Bahá. In a feature article that appeared on Sunday, May 5, she told her story:

It was near the dinner hour. I stopped for a moment [outside the Hotel Ansonia] to watch the well dressed, well fed looking crowd pass to and fro . . . everything moving at a high rate of speed.

I said to myself: "Well, of all the places to find the Master!" . . .

On my way to the more rarefied atmosphere of the upper floors I found myself hoping that the Baha would tell me I had a lovely soul. They say he finds out the strangest things about you. . . .

I felt all sorts of mystic possibilities awaited me the other side of the door. I stripped my mind of all its worldly debris. . . .

At my finger's pressure on the bell the door flew open with a most unholy speed.

No fumes of incense, no tinkling bells, no prostrate figures and whispered benedictions. . . .

Slipping into a ready chair, I looked about to find myself one of a concourse of people all actuated by the same interest.

My editor had given me the information that there

were five thousand Bahaites in America and about twenty million in the world, so why I should have expected to have the Baha all to myself I do not know, but I did.

I solaced my disappointment by studying the visitors, curious to learn what sort of people the faith drew to itself.

An enthusiastic, plump, middle-aged little person, gowned in a very worldly manner . . . was telling the stranger seated near of a domestic disturbance. . . .

My glance then carromed with a man who had sped down the corridor ahead of me.

He had flying coattails and a black sombrero, so I classified him as from the Middle West. . . .

After, several groups of foreigners, alert, silent, expectant, drew my regard. Many prosperous-looking business men and many interesting women.

There was a pretty girl on a narrow seat. You felt she must have lots of oversoul. She wore a sad, withdrawn look as of one who lives on the heights. A stout man, baldish, with a fringe of long hair on his neck, had the remaining two-thirds of the seat. . . .

Suddenly there was a stir, murmurs of "The Master!" Many stood up, a few rushed from the room. . . .

Abdul Baha entered.

He is scarcely above medium height, but so extraordinary is the dignity of his majestic carriage that he seemed more than the average stature. . . .

While slowly making the round of the room his soft, penetrating, faded eyes studied us all, without seeming to do so.

One and another he termed "My child!"—and they were not all young who responded to this greeting.

He stopped longest before the young girls and boys, those "blossoms on life's branch," as he speaks of them in Oriental imagery.

A blushing young woman introduced her escort—"Master, we have just been married."

Such a look of joy illumined the face that in repose looks like a sheet of parchment on which Fate has scored deep, cabalistic lines.

He did not want to leave them. He held their hands a long time, then turned and blessed the young man.

My dears, if that young man ever thinks of straying from the path of loyalty, methinks the pressure of that hand will weigh heavy on his soul.

He patted several people on the cheek, an old man, an apple-cheeked youth and myself. . . .

We seated ourselves about him. A good-looking young Turk understudying Dr. Fareed explained modestly: "You know it is very difficult to translate the Master literally. I can tell you the words, but no one could possibly interpret the beautiful soul that informs them."

Rather nice, that, I thought!

The Baha repeated a statement he had made that day to the students of Columbia University.

"The great need of this country is the spiritual philosophy, the philosophy of the language of God. Every one wants to find scientific truths, but we should seek the scientific truths of the spirit as well.

"Natural philosophy is like a very beautiful physical body, but the spiritual philosophy is the soul of that body. If this body unites with this spirit, then we have the highest perfect society.

"What God gives us in this world is for a time, our

body is for a time, our millions of dollars are for a time, our houses, our automobiles, the same. But the spiritual gifts of God are forever. The greatness of this world will come to an end, but the greatness of the spiritual world is eternal.

"Read history. See how emperors and kings came and went. Nothing is left. The kingdom of the world passes; the kingdom of God will endure." . . .

Some one interrogated him concerning the mission of the theatre.

He was much agitated at this question, and the young Turk explained:

"The Master says that he went to the theatre to-day where they show how Christ was crucified ('The Terrible Meek'). He saw the acts. He wept. It is more than one thousand, nine hundred years since that time. He was unable to help himself. Yes, he wept, and not only he, but many others wept, too."

I can imagine repeating his phrases to some of my clever friends, who would be sure to say:

"Why, that's as old as the hills. I don't see anything to make a fuss about in that."

But the time honored words, even repeated by an interpreter, are so fraught with the Baha's wonderful personality that they seem never to have been uttered before. His meaning is not couched in any esoteric phrases. Again and again he has disclaimed the possession of hidden lore. Again and again he has placed the attainments of the heart and soul above those of the mind.

After a few more questions and answers the meeting is declared adjourned. Abdul Baha arises and passes into the inner room, where he gives some private hearings.

No one starts to go. He has actually made New York people forget the dinner hour.

That in itself is a victory, I think. Don't you?

From my corner I wait my turn, again absorbed watching the human current.

Bride and bridegroom pass with ecstatic faces. Middle West smooths his dominant coattails. . . .

Newspaper people go in and out, Turks, Syrians, business men, domestic and society women. Children. . . .

As I respond to Dr. Fareed's signal and pass into the inner room I notice everywhere symptoms of departure. I get the impression of a large, masculine family migrating from one part of the world to another, bringing messages of good cheer and brotherly feeling. It is very inspiring.

I find the Baha seated in a comfortable easy chair at the bay window. Dr. Fareed sits near him as soon as I have taken my place. His beautiful voice, like a golden echo, follows close the termination of each sentence.

The master looks very spirituelle. He is in a relaxed attitude. . . . So much more akin to the spirit world than this does he seem that I find myself often addressing Dr. Fareed personally, referring to him in the third person.

"Do you think our luxury degenerate," I ask, "as in this great hotel?"

Abdul Baha strokes his long white beard.

"Luxury has a limit. Beyond that limit it is not commendable. There is such a thing as moderation. Men must be temperate in all things."

"Does the attention paid at present in this country to material things sadden you? Does it argue to you a lack of progress?"

"Your material civilization is very wonderful. If only you will allow divine idealism to keep pace with it there is great hope for general progress."

"Is there any way of making this life in a commercial city less crude for the young boy and girl?"

"It would be well to get them together and say, 'Young ladies, God has created you all human; isn't it a pity that you should pass your energy along animalistic lines? God has created you men and women in order that you may acquire his virtues, that you may progress in all the degrees, that you may be veritable angels, holy and sanctified.'"

"There are so many temptations put in their way," I murmur.

The Abdul Baha looks very sympathetic, but his singsong tones are relentlessly firm.

"Let them try a little of the delicacy of the spiritual world, the sweetness of its perfection and see which life is preferable. . . ."

I noticed a trembling of the eyelids and that the gestures of arranging his turban and stroking his beard were more nervously frequent. Dr. Fareed answered to my inquiry, "Shall I go now?"

"He has been giving of himself to every one since 7 o'clock this morning. I am a perfect physical wreck, but he is willing to go on indefinitely."

Abdul Baha opened the half-closed eyelids to say:

"I am going to the poor in the Bowery now. I love them."

I was invited to accompany them. The Baha met my assent with a most Chesterfieldian expression of pleasure.

Mr. Mills, president of the Bahaite Society in New York, had placed his car at the disposal of Abdul Baha.

Can you picture your Aunt Kate and Abdul Baha going to it, hand in hand, through the Ansonia corridors?

Perhaps the guests didn't gurgle and gasp! Perhaps!

I did feel rather conspicuous, but I braced myself with the thought of the universal brotherhood and really got along fairly well.

When we were seated in the machine, every inch of space taken by some member of the suite, I caught myself thinking what an amusing little anecdote I might make of this happening. Just then the Master said to me in a gentle but firm voice:

"Remember, you press people are the servants of the public. You interpret our words and acts to them. With you is a great responsibility. Please remember and please treat us seriously."

Often during the interview I had felt like saying: "You dear old man! You fine old gentleman!" I felt more than ever like it now.

As if anyone could hold up that pure white soul to ridicule.

There was another gasp of surprise at the Bowery Mission as, still hand in hand—he just wouldn't let me go—the Baha and I trotted through a lane composed of several score of society's members. A few of the young ladies had their arms filled with flowers, which afterward filled the automobile. Some four hundred men were present, belonging to the mission.

Just before the services were concluded I saw the courier stealthily approach the platform and hand the Baha a green baize bag.

Of course, I wasn't going to let that go on without finding out all about it, and to my whispered inquiry the Baha said, smilingly:

"Some little lucky bits I am going to distribute to the men."

What you don't expect!

I had the surprise of my life!

For what do you suppose those lucky bits were?

Silver quarters, two hundred dollars' worth of them! There!

Guess you didn't expect it, either.

Think of it! Some one actually coming to America and distributing money. Not here with the avowed or unavowed intention of taking it away.

It seems incredible.

Possibly I may be a little tired of mere words, dealing in them the way I do, but that demonstration of Abdul Baha's creed did more to convince me of the absolute sincerity of the man than anything else that had happened.

And it was all done so unostentatiously, so gracefully, without any fuss or fume.

The Master stood, his eyes always turned away from the man facing him, far down the line, four or five beyond his vis-à-vis, so that when a particularly desperate looking specimen came along he was all ready for him, and, instead of one quarter, two were quietly pressed into the calloused palm.

Once a young Turk of the suite slipped in, and before the Baha recognized him got a coin. He explained that he wanted it for luck, and the Baha most benignly patted his shoulder. When he got back to his companions they all laughed at the joke.

I imagine them a merry little family among themselves.

I had said good night on the platform, so my last view of Abdul Baha was as he stood at the head of the Bowery Mission line, a dozen or more derelicts before him, giving to each a bit of silver and a word of blessing.

And as I went out into the starlight night I murmured the phrase of an Oriental admirer who had described him as

The *Breeze of God*.

The Bowery meeting had not been a last-minute arrangement. The preceding February, at the invitation of the mission minister, a Bahá'í had begun holding meetings there. When it was definite that 'Abdu'l-Bahá was coming to America, the men at the mission learned of it through Juliet Thompson and voted to ask Him to speak to them.

'Abdu'l-Bahá began His talk by saying, "Tonight I am very happy for I have come here to meet my friends. I consider you my relatives, my companions. . . ." He concluded, ". . . I ask you to accept Abdul Baha as your servant."[15]

After the talk, 'Abdu'l-Bahá and His small party took taxis back to the hotel. Looking at the glittering electric lights of Broadway, He smiled and mentioned that Bahá'u'lláh loved light. As the group walked along the hotel corridor to His rooms, they passed the chambermaid to whom He had given flowers earlier. This time He stopped her, had her hold out her apron, and dumped into it the quarters left over from the Bowery. Mr. John G.

Grundy, the last in line, stopped and explained how the quarters had been used; the maid replied, "'I will do the same with this money. I will give away every cent of it.'"[16]

'Abdu'l-Bahá's party ate a late supper in His rooms, and He talked about the play they had seen that afternoon and told them of scenes that should be added to make the story of Christ's crucifixion complete. They moved into another room and were talking about the Bowery meeting, when the maid came in and went straight to 'Abdu'l-Bahá, her eyes full of tears, bade Him good-bye, asked Him to pray for her, hid her face in her apron, and ran out of the room.[17]

On Friday, April 19, 'Abdu'l-Bahá spoke in Earl Hall at Columbia University, telling his audience, "it is our duty to put forth our greatest efforts and summon all our energies in order that the bonds of unity and accord may be established among mankind."[18]

That evening, Maḥmúd noted, "most of the friends stayed longer in His presence" and they "continued coming until late in the night." Because it was His last day in New York before leaving for Washington and Chicago the friends wanted to be with Him as long as possible.

3

Washington, D.C.

Elbert Hubbard, one of the major newspaper colum-
nists of the period, later wrote:

> When he ['Abdu'l-Bahá] went to Washington, and
> swept through the Capitol, even the Supreme Court of
> the United States saw fit to adjourn; the House the
> same; and the Senate, for a while, at least, forgot mat-
> ters of investigation.
> When Abdul Baha went to the White House one
> might have thought that he was going with the intent to
> take possession of it.
> But his is not a kingdom of this world, so far as a
> desire to rule is concerned. . . .[1]

The *Washington Bee* noted, on April 27, "Its [the Bahá'í
Faith's] white devotees, even in this prejudice-ridden
community, refuse to draw the color line. The informal
meetings, held frequently in the fashionable mansions of
the cultured society in Sheridan Circle, Dupont Circle,
Connecticut and Massachusetts avenues, have been open
to Negroes on terms of absolute equality."

'Abdu'l-Bahá arrived in Washington, D.C., on Saturday, April 20—His tenth day in America—and left on Sunday, April 28. It was a week of ceaseless activity. His train arrived at the Pennsylvania Railroad Station at 1:33 P.M., after a five-hour trip. He had already let the Washington friends know that He did not wish the hour of His arrival announced nor any delegation sent. Ali-Kuli Khan and his family and the officers of the Persian-American Society met Him, and He went to the waiting car of Mrs. Barney-Hemmick.

Mrs. Arthur J. Parsons had for some time been supplicating 'Abdu'l-Bahá to reside at her Washington home, but He had not accepted. The friends who met Him pleaded with Him to stay with her, saying that Mrs. Parsons had built the house for the purpose of His visit and that she would be dejected if He refused. For her sake, He accepted and went with an interpreter to her home, sending the others in His group to a house which He had already rented.

Saturday night He spoke to the Persian-American Society, with six hundred people packed into a public library hall that normally seated four hundred. At least one hundred more standing outside took off their hats as 'Abdu'l-Bahá approached. The audience in the auditorium rose to its feet as soon as He entered and stood until He bade them be seated. The next day the *Washington Evening Star* reported that "after he had spoken and when he was seated on the platform, hundreds pressed around him, seeking to grasp his hand."

Included in the group were reporters who asked His opinions of the *Titanic* disaster. They reported that He said, "'Both Americans and Europeans seem to be possessed of the mania for speed. . . . It was a pitiful waste of life that came because of the effort to save a few hours in time—rushing a great vessel at top speed when it was known there was danger from ice.'"[2]

On Sunday morning, April 21, ceaseless streams of people were drawn toward His house as if by a magnet. At 11:15 A.M., He went to Studio Hall at 1219 Connecticut Avenue and spoke to more than two hundred people.

At 4:00 P.M. He spoke at the Universalist Church at 13th and L Streets to more than one thousand persons, who had started filling the auditorium an hour before time for the service to begin. In introducing Him the Reverend John Van Schaick, Jr., pastor of the church, said, "After arrangements for this meeting had been made, I received a letter warning me that I should be false to my belief if I held it. . . . Against such narrowness this Church has always stood. We stand today humbly seeking the Spirit of Truth. . . ."[3] 'Abdu'l-Bahá then addressed the gathering:

> . . . The doctrines and creed of this church so capably expressed by its revered minister are truly commendable. . . . It is evident that prejudices arising from adherence to religious forms and imitation of ancestral beliefs have hindered the progress of humanity thousands of years. . . .
>
> Now it is enough! We must investigate reality. . . .[4]

At the conclusion, most of the audience remained for a spontaneous informal reception.

Every afternoon at 5:00 P.M., from Monday through Friday, receptions were held at the Parsons' home, to which hundreds of Washington diplomats, scientists, and socially prominent persons came. On Monday, April 22, to the dignitaries, 'Abdu'l-Bahá explained:

> Some movements appear, manifest a brief period of activity, then discontinue. Others show forth a greater measure of growth and strength, but before attaining mature development, weaken, disintegrate and are lost in oblivion. . . . There is still another kind of movement or cause which from a very small, inconspicuous beginning goes forward with sure and steady progress, gradually broadening and widening until it has assumed universal dimensions. The Bahai movement is of this nature.[5]

On Tuesday morning, April 23, well over a thousand students, faculty members, administrators, and guests jammed Rankin Chapel when 'Abdu'l-Bahá presented His memorable address at Howard University. Maḥmúd noted, "here, as elsewhere, when both white and colored people were present, Abdul Baha seemed happiest." He was introduced by the President of the University as "the prophet of peace and the herald of love and prosperity." 'Abdu'l-Bahá dramatically proclaimed, "the accomplishment of unity between the colored and whites will be an assurance of the world's peace."[6] The ovation He received brought Him forward again to acknowledge it. The people surged outside and stood in two ranks on either side of Him as He passed by.

From Howard University He rode to the Persian Embassy, where Ali-Kuli Khan was preparing a reception. 'Abdu'l-Bahá went upstairs to rest and to grant a few private interviews, including conversations with Admiral Peary and Alexander Graham Bell. Mrs. Hebe Struven, who helped arrange the affair, recalling it years later, said that after the place cards had been arranged at the plates to seat people by strict Washington protocol, 'Abdu'l-Bahá at the last minute gathered them all up, shuffled and redistributed them, and then brought Louis G. Gregory to the place of honor at the head of the table in the otherwise all-white gathering. He thus—literally in this gathering and symbolically for all occasions—abolished racial prejudice and social segregation.

Admiral Peary had just been credited, after controversy with another contender, with being the first person to reach the North Pole. 'Abdu'l-Bahá told him at the reception that, since the world had been concerned with what was at the pole for so long, by discovering there was nothing there, he had relieved the public mind and rendered a great service. Admiral Peary was nonplussed.[7]

Yúsuf Díyá Páshá, the Turkish Minister, was there, representing the country that had for so long been associated with 'Abdu'l-Bahá's imprisonment. He listened in rapt attention as 'Abdu'l-Bahá spoke and turned to one of the Bahá'ís saying, "'This is irrefutable. This is pure logic.'"[8]

The Parsons' reception began soon after the Embassy reception ended, and observers noted that 'Abdu'l-Bahá entered the Parsons' home holding the hand of Díyá Páshá. Referring to the recent sinking of the *Titanic*, He told those present:

I was greatly affected by this disaster. Some of those who were lost, voyaged on the 'Cedric' with us as far as Naples and afterwards sailed upon the other ship. When I think of them I am very sad indeed. But when I consider this calamity in another aspect, I am consoled

by the realization that the worlds of God are infinite. . . .[9]

Juliet Thompson wrote of this meeting in an entry in her
diary on May 7:

Into this room of conventional elegance, packed with
conventional people, imagine the Master striding with
His free step, walking first to one of the many windows
and, while He looked out into the light, talking with
His matchless ease to the people. Turning from the
window, striding back and forth with a step so vibrant it
shook you. Piercing our souls with those strange eyes
—uplifting them, glory streaming upon them. Talking,
talking, moving to and fro incessantly. Pushing back
His turban, revealing that Christ-like forehead; pushing it forward again almost down to His eyebrows,
which gave Him a peculiar majesty. Charging, *filling*
the room with magnetic currents, with a mysterious
energy.

At the end of the Parsons' reception 'Abdu'l-Bahá went
to Washington and M Street N.W. to the large Metropolitan African Methodist Episcopal Church, where the auditorium was taxed to capacity with people waiting to hear
Him speak to the Bethel Literary and Historical Society, to
which He afterward made a contribution. Late that night,
before going to rest, 'Abdu'l-Bahá told the friends, "'We
must offer thanks to the Blessed Beauty, because it is His
help that has stirred the people. . . .'"
On Wednesday morning, April 24, 'Abdu'l-Bahá spoke
at Studio Hall at a reception for children which opened

with songs by the children. He told the parents, "Know ye the value of these children for they are all my children."[10] He chanted a prayer especially for them, embraced each child, and gave each a piece of candy.

He then attended another of the daily receptions at the Parsons' home, after which He proceeded to 13th Street N.W. to the home of Andrew J. Dyer. In his diary, Dr. Zia Bagdadi, who served as one of 'Abdu'l-Bahá's translators, wrote, "In the evening, 'Abdu'l-Bahá addressed the white and colored believers and their friends at the home of Mrs. Dyer, a member of the colored race. . . ."[11] 'Abdu'l-Bahá concluded His address by saying, "When the racial elements of the American nation unite in actual fellowship and accord, the lights of the oneness of humanity will shine, the day of eternal glory and bliss will dawn, the spirit of God encompass and the divine favors descend. . . . This is the sign of the 'Most Great Peace;' . . ."[12]

In the late evening 'Abdu'l-Bahá left the Dyers' and took a streetcar to go to the home of Alexander Graham Bell. Maḥmúd recalled that "He was very happy this day and was talking so loudly that His voice was heard over the din and noise of the tramcar. He said, '. . . O Bahá'u'lláh! How merciful art Thou! In what persecutions you spent your days! What troubles you suffered! But what solid foundations you laid! What a manifest standard you unfurled!'"

Alexander Graham Bell had assembled his friends and fellow scientists in his home so that they might meet 'Abdu'l-Bahá. He spoke to them and answered their questions on science and other matters until midnight, when a late meal was served. Bell explained, as he introduced his wife, who was deaf and dumb, that through his efforts to develop a hearing device he invented the telephone. 'Abdu'l-Bahá indicated that many discoveries came about in the same way, noting that many medicines came from alchemy and that America was discovered during the search for a route to the East. 'Abdu'l-Bahá stayed overnight as a guest of the Bells.

On Thursday, April 25, a large delegation from the Theosophical Society arrived at the Parsons' home at 10:30 A.M. They had barely departed when a group of Esperantists came. He told them, "The heart is like a box and language is the key."[13] By the afternoon when the crowds were pouring into the Parsons' home for the daily reception, 'Abdu'l-Bahá joked with Mrs. Parsons, "'It is very difficult to have one like me as a guest. Every guest and traveler has a limited number of friends with whom he makes special dates for visits, but you are forced all day long to be the entertainer of all.'"[14]

That evening Díyá Páshá held a large reception for 'Abdu'l-Bahá at the Turkish Embassy. Roses had been piled along the tables and formed a mound in the center where 'Abdu'l-Bahá and Díyá Páshá sat. Díyá Páshá watched his guest with eyes filled at times with tears. In his address welcoming 'Abdu'l-Bahá, he said, "'Your Holiness has suffered great persecution and troubles for the sake of propagating the virtues of human morality. . . . 'Abdu'l-Bahá is a peerless being of the age. . . .'" When the affair was ended, Díyá Páshá walked 'Abdu'l-Bahá to the streetcar stop. After 'Abdu'l-Bahá returned to the Parsons', former President of the United States Theodore Roosevelt came to see Him.

Among the visitors on Friday morning, April 26, was Lee McClung, the Secretary of the Treasury of the United States. Later 'Abdu'l-Bahá addressed the ladies of President Taft's All Saints Unitarian Church; the room was completely filled. After the daily Parsons' reception He took a walk in the park. That evening He spoke to another capacity crowd, in one of the largest halls in Washington—the Continental Hall of the Daughters of the American Revolution—sharing the platform with Samuel Gompers, the president of the American Federation of Labor, Benjamin Trueblood, secretary of the American Peace Society, and A. C. Monohan of the United States Bureau of Education.

'Abdu'l-Bahá, Who kept the friends in the Holy Land and Persia apprised of the activities through frequent cablegrams, cabled, "'This day three thousand persons were interviewed in utmost harmony.'"

'Abdu'l-Bahá had breakfast on Saturday morning, April 27, with Treasurer McClung, who embraced Him and wept when they parted. At the Parsons' reception in the afternoon He said to a Justice of the Supreme Court, "'It is possible to establish such unity among the powers of the whole world as is found in the United States of America.'"

To some of the doctors He said, "'I hope that you will raise the standard of the universal peace.'"

To a mathematician He said, "'I hope that you will try to teach the truth and principles of divine religions to different nations as you are teaching mathematics to different persons in your school.'"

To Admiral Peary He said, "'I hope that you will explore the invisibilities of the Kingdom.'"

To the Archbishop He said, "'I hope you will throw away the injurious formalism, enforce the truth of the teachings of Christ, and remove all those dogmas that are against science and reality.'"

To the Chargé d'Affaires of Switzerland He spoke of His visit to that country the year before.

To some relatives of the President He spoke of the divine civilization.

To a member of Congress He said, "'As you are endeavoring for the good of America, so you must put forth your energy for the good of the whole world and all the nations.'"

He asked a Supreme Court Judge what the verdict was. "It is all right," said the Judge, and 'Abdu'l-Bahá smiled.

"Let him ['Abdu'l-Bahá] visit any bank, factory, office building, church," Elbert Hubbard wrote later, "and everything is laid aside, and eyes bulge and ears listen until he takes his departure."[15]

On April 28, at 5:30 P.M., 'Abdu'l-Bahá left Washington for His first visit to Chicago.

4

Chicago

"BAHAIST CHIEF MISSING," proclaimed the Monday, April 29, *Chicago Daily News*. Amidst news that, in the Kimmel case, Kimmel was trying to regain his lost memory; that experiments with mice would stop cancer; that Japan's influence in Mexico was causing U.S. concern; that Taft and Roosevelt were beginning to campaign during this presidential election year; and that there was an "open war" to "make Chicago clean," the newspaper asked:

> Where is Abdul-Baha, son of Baha'o'llah, . . . who was coming to Chicago to-day to preach the universal brotherhood of man?
> Chicago Bahaists—there are said to be some 40,000,000 followers in the world—asked each other this question and failed to find an answer. In the Corinthian hall in the Masonic Temple building 170 delegates attending the Bahai convention waited for the leader of the movement.

'Abdu'l-Bahá arrived on Monday evening, April 29, His nineteenth day in America, and drove to the Plaza

47

Hotel next to Lincoln Park. The phone was already ringing with calls from reporters requesting interview time.
"'Tomorrow morning,'" 'Abdu'l-Bahá told them. To the
friends in His hotel suite, He reported:

> In Washington we always had one thousand and
> two thousand hearers in large meetings. Day and night
> I had no rest. A close friendship has been created be-
> tween the colored and white friends. They have be-
> come excellent believers. Even those, who have not
> become believers, have become much nearer. Notwith-
> standing all this, I like Chicago more, because the first
> voice of Bahá'u'lláh was raised from this city.

It was a warm, springlike day on Tuesday, April 30,
when Jane Addams welcomed 'Abdu'l-Bahá to Hull
House and introduced Him to an audience that far ex-
ceeded the auditorium's seating capacity of 750.
'Abdu'l-Bahá spoke on the unity of the races, saying,
"God is not pleased with, neither should any reasonable or
intelligent man be willing to recognize inequality in the
races because of this distinction [color]."[1] Concerning
racial conditions in Chicago, Maḥmúd noted, "Dr. Zia
Bagdadi invited Mr. Gregory . . . to his home. The
owner of the house, hearing this, came to Dr. Zia and
asked him very seriously to vacate the house because the
Doctor had given a colored man access to his home. In
such surging waves of hatred and prejudice the influence
of the divine Cause and the power of the Covenant of God
was . . . victorious. . . ." As 'Abdu'l-Bahá left Hull
House, many children and unemployed men crowded
around to meet Him; to each He gave coins.

From Hull House He went by car to Handel Hall to speak to the Fourth Annual Convention of the National Association for the Advancement of Colored People, which had been discussing lynchings and job and housing discrimination. He said to the assemblage:

Can we apply the test of racial color and say that man of a certain hue—white, black, brown, yellow, red—is the true image of his creator? We must conclude that color is not the standard and estimate of judgment and that it is of no importance. . . . Therefore be it known that color or race is of no importance. . . . Man is not man simply because of bodily attributes. The standard of divine measure and judgment is his intelligence and spirit.[2]

From Handel Hall 'Abdu'l-Bahá went to Drill Hall in the Masonic Temple where two thousand people rose as He entered. He spoke to them about building the Bahá'í House of Worship, but He did not mention the $9,000 that the newspaper reported trustees of the Temple Unity Committee had agreed to raise. He told them, instead, "The real temple is the very Word of God. . . . Temples are the symbols of the divine uniting force. . . . The outer edifice is a symbol of the inner. May the people be admonished thereby. . . ."[3]

The Chicago newspapers continued their reports, with varying degrees of accuracy. The *Chicago Examiner* said:

Prophet Abdul Baha Here. . . .
. . . Abdul Baha is in Chicago, making this city temporarily the capital of a religious movement that is

said to have 15,000,000 followers throughout the world.

. . . With women gowned in blue robes and turbans, the men garbed in flowing robes and fezzes, his rooms had the appearance of an Oriental court.

. . . His eyes . . . flashed the vigor of a man who . . . might be said to have no age. . . .

The *Chicago Daily News* reported:

Without the door of the Plaza hotel suite a dish of radishes and celery, sprinkled with water, was discovered. This was part of the breakfast of Abdul Baha. . . .

"A reporter must be a purveyor of truth," he said. . . . "The newspapers are leaders of the people and the people must be able to rely on what they read. Now, some reporter on a Chicago morning newspaper said that I wore a gown and turban with red and white stripes. I never wore such colors. He said my beard reached to my waist. Look at it."

The beard, in truth, came scarcely to the chest. . . .

The *Chicago Inter-Ocean* said, "WORLD HARMONY IS AIM OF ABDUL-BAHA":

Abdul-Baha, leader of 40,000,000 Bahaists, was interviewed yesterday at the Plaza hotel, temporarily turned into an oriental court. . . .

The newspapers also noted that Harvard would cut down its elms after commencement because of elm tree beetles; that 116 *Titanic* victims were buried at sea and that a ship was returning with 190 bodies; that Marconi and Caruso sailed from America on a "safeguarded" liner; that playwright August Strindberg was dying of cancer; and that a maximum automobile speed limit of fifteen to twenty miles an hour had been proposed.

On Wednesday, May 1, the day 'Abdu'l-Bahá was to lay the foundation stone for the first Bahá'í House of Worship in the Western Hemisphere, weather forecasters in the *Chicago Daily News* predicted unsettled conditions "and probably occasional showers to-night." A marquee tent had been set up on the Temple site, with three hundred chairs arranged in nine sections separated by aisles leading to a central open area. A special entryway had been prepared for 'Abdu'l-Bahá's carriage in the middle of the eastern side of the tract. He arrived, instead, by taxi and entered on the northern side. Pacing back and forth before the filled chairs and two hundred additional persons who were standing, He spoke of the importance of the Mashriqu'l-Adhkár. [4]

A newspaper reporter covering the dedication for the *Chicago Daily News* noted:

> The Persian broke off when he noticed one of those in the crowd shiver. "I'm afraid you are cold," he said.
>
> "We're not!" called back several members of the crowd.
>
> "Then you are denizens of Chicago," smiled the Persian leader.

They moved outside the tent and spadefuls of earth were turned by persons from Persia, Syria, Egypt, India,

Japan, South Africa, England, France, Germany, Holland, Norway, Sweden, and Denmark and by North American Indians; 'Abdu'l-Bahá finished the effort and placed the stone. The *Daily News* reported that the audience sang,

> "May we now receive His spirit,
>   And its radiance shed afar.
> Now and here in love abiding,
>   In the realm of El-Ab-Ha."

Then, the report continued, "The ceremony through, the crowds formed two lines from the tent to the waiting taxicab. Abdul Baha moved down the lane and stepped into the machine. A moment later his creamy fez was nodding farewell."

"Believe Abdul Baha May Be Second Dowie—Zionists Ask Cult Leader to Visit Colony; See Possible Fulfillment of Prophecy," proclaimed the *Chicago Examiner* on Thursday, May 2. The article explained:

> Asserting their belief that the mantle of the late John Alexander Dowie may have descended upon Abdul Baha . . . followers of the Dowie Church in Zion City invited Baha to visit their colony to-day. . . .
>
> "Nineteen hundred and twelve is the year during which, according to Dr. Dowie's prediction, a new prophet is to appear in Zion," said Deveraux [of Zion]. "We believe that Baha may be the teacher who is appointed to lead us out of our troubles."

The article added, "Abdul Baha accepted an invitation to

In Front of Riverside Park, New York, 1912

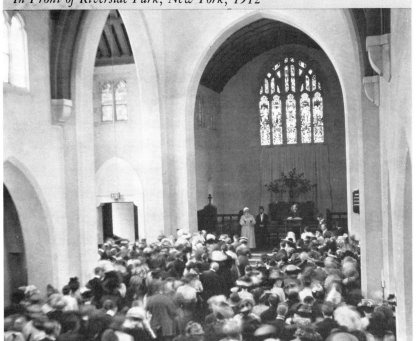

Speaking in Plymouth Congregational Church,
Chicago, May 5, 1912

With a Group of Bahá'ís in Lincoln Park, Chicago, 1912

Seated on a Bench in Lincoln Park,
Chicago, 1912

'Abdu'l-Bahá Addressing Delegates and Friends
to the Fourth Annual Bahá'í Convention
on the Occasion of His Laying the Cornerstone
of the Bahá'í House of Worship,
Wilmette, Illinois, May 1, 1912

address a meeting of suffrage workers this evening at Hotel LaSalle. 'I believe in suffrage for women,' he said, 'but no, it should not be striven for by window-smashing, and by what are called militant methods.'"

Before leaving for the suffrage meeting 'Abdu'l-Bahá spoke to the successive waves of people who came to His hotel. Some He saw individually, and some He talked to in groups in the Large Parlor that could hold 150 at a time (a room which the management had put at His disposal), dismissing them so more people waiting outside could enter.

The ballroom at the LaSalle was filled with more than a thousand women of the federated clubs whom He addressed on the equality of women. A second meeting closely followed the first, for the Bahá'í women had invited all of the women's clubs' representatives to a reception in 'Abdu'l-Bahá's honor in the same ballroom. Ten speakers praised Him, and then He spoke again.

The editorial page of the *Chicago Inter-Ocean* that evening picked up an earlier story as it cryptically stated, "Abdul-Baha . . . feels a little doubtful of our newspapers because a reporter wrote that he wore a robe and turban of red and white stripes—which he never did; so there!" The newspaper also reported that in baseball, the Chicago Cubs, in their initial appearance in Pittsburgh, won over the Pirates 7 to 2, while the Sox lost to the Tigers in Detroit, 5 to 2.

On Friday, May 3, the papers chronicled the news that twenty-three were indicted for a lynching in Fort Smith, Arkansas; that England had ordered sixty "aeroplanes"; that an Oklahoma tornado destroyed a small town; that a two hundred mile section in the Panama Canal zone was

affected by an earthquake, although work on the canal
continued; and that a tidal wave near Australia had destroyed a Fiji Island village.

Among the streams of visitors to His hotel came a group
of persons from India now resident in Chicago; their
leader read 'Abdu'l-Bahá a statement of welcome:

> Sir:
>
> We the members of the Indian Club of Chicago wel-
> come you to this country. . . . The Bahá'í Cause, like
> the cause of Buddha, will be a source of uniting
> nations. . . .
>
> . . . we believe that our country, India, will be
> greatly benefited by a visit from your Excellency. The
> lack of unity between Hindus and Muhammedans
> has kept them in utmost contention and strife. But as
> your Excellency's teachings are very much like the
> teachings of our religious leaders, they will undoubt-
> edly unite them and make these contending nations
> one. We hope that your Excellency will be received
> with the same warmth and enthusiasm in India as here
> in America. . . .

'Abdu'l-Bahá often walked in the morning and evening
through Lincoln Park and through the zoo, taking the
friends with Him and talking on the way, sometimes
allowing the friends to take photographs of Him. At times
He picked up a stick as He walked, using it like a cane.
The friends recalled how, as He stood seemingly absorbed in watching the polar bear, they tiptoed back out of
camera range as the photographer positioned himself for a
profile view, without asking 'Abdu'l-Bahá. But just as he
was about to click the shutter, 'Abdu'l-Bahá laughed and

playfully hit him across the back of the neck with a light touch of the cane.

From the zoo He led the friends toward the lake, sat on a bench, motioned the friends to do likewise, and discussed unity with them. He said, "'Some of you may have observed that I have not called attention to any of your individual shortcomings. I would suggest to you, that if you shall be similarly considerate in your treatment of each other, it will be greatly conducive to the harmony of your association with each other. . . .'"⁵

Maḥmúd noted:

At night there was a consultation meeting of the Bahá'ís. He sent us there and later He came Himself. After giving a brief discourse He left for the hotel. In the matter of Mashriqu'l-Adhkár, He said that He did not wish to interfere. It was the business of the consultation board. At another time, He said, "If I were to speak about Mashriqu'l-Adhkár, it would be built at once."

The weekend newspapers told of newspaper strikers beating newsboys; of the flooding Mississippi River killing several people; of a third son born to John D. Rockefeller; of proposals to put highway tunnels under the Hudson River; and of a "suffrage army" of ten thousand, marching and demonstrating for women's voting rights.

On Saturday, May 4, 'Abdu'l-Baha spoke to the Theosophists at Northwestern University in Evanston. On Sunday, He especially invited the children to be brought to the Large Parlor. He talked to each one of them, held them in His lap, embracing and kissing them, whispering in their ears. One observer wrote, "The children's joy and his own happiness seemed to culminate when one dear little tot ran to him and fairly threw herself into his arms. When he let her go she stood for a second and then suddenly laughed aloud with perfect joy. . . ."[6] He told them, "You are all my children, my spiritual children."[7] He took a bouquet of flowers from the center table and divided it among the children and gave each one an envelope of rose petals, as He spoke to each individually again. Then He took them all out into the park for photographs. After a time He expressed His wish to be alone and walked over to the statue of Abraham Lincoln and stood gazing up at it.

At 11:00 A.M. He spoke at the Plymouth Congregational Church on East 50th Street. The Reverend Joseph A. Milburn introduced Him: "'Having heard of the teachings of the peerless qualities of 'Abdu'l-Bahá, I had made arrangements to leave for 'Akká. Then I was informed that 'Abdu'l-Bahá, Himself, was coming to America. God has today endowed a great blessing upon us that 'Abdu'l-Bahá has graced us with His presence here.'" As 'Abdu'l-Bahá came forward, the audience stood, and, even though in a church sanctuary, they burst into prolonged cheers that stopped only when He motioned them to silence. Some of the audience at this and other meetings became so attracted to Him, even though they had just met Him, that they followed Him from meeting to meeting.

'Abdu'l-Bahá lunched with Dr. Forde and afterward started back to the hotel. 'Abdu'l-Bahá suggested that they walk part of the distance and then take a streetcar. The friends insisted that they all ride in Dr. Forde's car, to which 'Abdu'l-Bahá submitted. But the car had two flat tires on the way, and they ended up taking the streetcar.

On Sunday evening 'Abdu'l-Bahá spoke to the All-Souls

Church. The meeting was held, since the congregation had no building of its own, at the Abraham Lincoln Center at 700 East Oakwood, a building with a seating capacity of seven hundred. Afterward He went to the home of Dr. Melborne before returning to the hotel.

On Monday morning, May 6, He left Chicago for Cleveland. Maḥmúd noted, "Bahá'ís and non-Bahá'ís were surrounding Him like moths. . . ."

5

Cleveland,
Pittsburgh,
Washington, D.C.

"GIVES NEW CREED TALK," said the May 5 *Cleveland Plain Dealer*, in anticipation of the Master's visit, adding, "Abd-ul Baha. . . . comes to Cleveland from Chicago, where his ardent followers recently dedicated a temple. . . . It is expected a branch will be formed here."

The next day another article in the same paper, headed "BAHAISTS TO HEAR VENERABLE LEADER," noted:

> There are a number of followers of the Bahaist movement in Cleveland. Converts are expected as a result of the visit of Abdul Baha. Some Cleveland believers went to Chicago last week to the dedication of the Bahaist temple. . . .
>
> . . . .
>
> The business affairs of the Baha movement are conducted by assemblies of consultation. It is expected eventually there will be a general assembly composed of representatives from all parts of the world. This will be known as "The Universal House of Justice."*

*The Universal House of Justice was first elected in 1963 by members of the fifty-six National Spiritual Assemblies in countries around the world; it resides at the Bahá'í World Center, Haifa, Israel.

The friends and reporters met 'Abdu'l-Bahá at the train station when He arrived at 4:00 P.M. on May 6. He checked into rooms at the Hotel Euclid and talked to the reporters, and an hour later went to Dr. C. M. Swingle's home to talk to the Bahá'ís.

He then returned to the Hotel for a public meeting attended by some five hundred people, many of whom had to stand. Afterward, a number of them, including reporters, followed Him to His rooms and asked Him questions on various subjects, including intermarriage. This latter discussion caused front-page headlines the next day.

The *Cleveland News* article stated:

WED RACES? SURE. . . .
"Perfect results follow the marriage of black and white races. All men are the progeny of one. . . . They are of different colors, but the color is nothing."—Abdul Baha. . . .
"I believe Abdul Baha is absolutely right. It is inevitable that all races will unite. Black and white and yellow will intermarry and make one perfect race. It is the only logical conclusion."—Mrs. C. M. Swingle.

The *Cleveland Plain Dealer* reported, "BAHAIST AP-PROVES UNIONS OF RACES: Persian Teacher Tells Cleveland Women Intermarriage Results Ideal." The article, which ran the length of the front page and concluded on page three with several column inches of photographs, stated:

Abdul Baha, a venerable Persian now touring America as leader of the Bahaist movement for a universal religion, declared last night for an amalgamation of the white and negro races by intermarriage. . . .

"All men," said Abdul Baha, "are progeny of one—Adam. They are of different color, but color is nothing. Men of all races are brothers. God is neither black nor white. . . ."

"Perfect results follow the marriage of black and white races. In my own family in Persia was a negro slave who was freed. She married a white man and her children married white men. These children are now in my household. The results of the union were beautiful. They were wonderful—perfect."

Abdul Baha's talk was in Persian, as was his lecture. Sentence by sentence, as he proceeded, it was translated into English by Dr. Ameer Fareed, also a Persian.

. . . .

There was no churchy pomp in his ['Abdu'l-Bahá's] manner, either on his arrival in Cleveland, when he addressed his audience or when he received the disciples who came to his apartments. His manner was one of benevolence and gentle humility.

When he sat at one side of the crowded hotel lobby early in the evening he gazed over it sadly, as if in melancholy contemplation of the lack of spirituality he found in all the material civilization of America. He sat with his hand to his forehead.

When he talked to those who found him in his apartment his face lighted with smiles. But all the time his aspect of venerable benevolence was curiously joined to an expression and manner so simple and unaffected that it seemed almost childlike.

Another aged Persian, Mirza Mohmoad, was one of the Bahaist messiah's party. There were four of them,

Abdul Baha Abbas, Dr. Ameer Fareed, Mirza Mohmoad and Said Assadullah.

Dr. E. C. Getsinger, Mrs. Getsinger, and Mrs. W.
C. Ralston, all of Cleveland, had attended the meetings
in Chicago and accompanied the party to Cleveland.
The Cleveland followers of the Bahaist movement
number about 100. Several met the party at Union
station. From there automobiles carried Abdul Baha
and the others to the home of Dr. C. M. Swingle at 8203
Wade Park-av N.E. where about forty had gathered for
a reception. . . .

That Abdul Baha's approval of marriages between
white and negroes is but a natural part of his movement
for a universal religion was indicated by extracts from a
stenographic report of his sermon.

"Humanity," he said, "will be bound together as one.
The various religions shall be united and the various
races shall be known as one kind."

This is to be when the spiritual civilization which the
Bahaist movement is to bring about is achieved.

"The material civilization," he said, "has now
reached its pitch, and there is need for a spiritual civilization. Material civilization alone will not satisfy. Its
benefits are limited to the world of matter.

"There is no hindrance for the spirit of man, for spirit
itself must progress, and if the divine civilization shall
be organized, then the spirit will advance.

"Real discoveries will then take place. The divine
mysteries will be revealed. The power of the Holy
Spirit will become effective. The influence of the great
guidance will be experienced, and all that is conducive
to the divine form of civilization. That is what is meant
in the Bible by the descent of the New Jerusalem. The

heavenly Jerusalem is no other than the divine civilization, and it is now ready. It can be and shall be organized, and the oneness of humankind will be a fact.

"Humanity will then be bound together as one. The
various religions shall be united, and the various races
shall be known as one kind. The Orient and the Occi-
dent shall be united and the banner of international
peace shall be unfurled. The world shall find peace and
the equality and rights of men shall be established. All
the nations of the world shall then be relatives and
companions."

On May 7, 'Abdu'l-Bahá left at 8:00 A.M. for Pittsburgh, arriving about noon, and went with the friends to
His rooms in the Hotel Schenley. One by one He talked to
them privately. Among other things, they kept asking
Him if He liked the rooms. He told each of them, "'Very
good! Very good!'" After they had departed, He turned to
Dr. Zia Bagdadi and exclaimed:

The friends here are anxious to know if I like these
rooms! They do not know what we had to go through in
the past. Imagine the conditions and surroundings
when we were . . . imprisoned in the barracks of
'Akká; Bahá'u'lláh occupied one room; His family and
several other families were forced to occupy one room.
Aside from the severe illness that was raging, and the
death of many among us prisoners—adults and
children—on account of unsanitary surroundings and
starvation, I noticed that my own presence in that
crowded room was another source of torture to all of
them. This was due to the fact that parents and children
were suppressing and restraining themselves by trying

to be quiet and polite in my presence. So, in order to give them freedom, I accepted the morgue of the barracks, because that was the only room available, and I lived in it for about two years. Now the kind friends here wish to know if I like these magnificent rooms![1]

He then went to a public meeting in the hotel and afterward spoke more informally with a number of doctors and educators who had come.

On Wednesday, May 8, after early morning tea, 'Abdu'l-Bahá packed, and caught the 9:00 A.M. train for a second visit to Washington, D.C. His companions begged Him to take a special compartment or a berth on the train; but He refused saying, "'I spend money only to help people and to serve the Cause of God; and I have never liked distinctions since my childhood.'"

After a twelve-hour train ride they arrived in Washington; but this time 'Abdu'l-Bahá refused Mrs. Parsons' invitation to stay in her home. Instead He rented an apartment at 1340 Harvard Street. From there He went to the Parsons' home where there was an assemblage of people waiting for Him.

On Thursday, May 9, people came to Him all day long. Many ministers invited Him to speak in their churches. When a few spoke against Him, He observed, "'I deal with people very gently that they may not turn away and raise the least objection. Yet these ministers have accused us of atheism. . . .'"[2]

On Friday, May 10, He spoke at a women's meeting, visited a settlement house for children, and went to Mrs. Alice Barney's for supper, where He talked late into the night. The next day 'Abdu'l-Bahá left Washington.

6

New York,
New Jersey,
Massachusetts

When 'Abdu'l-Bahá arrived in New York on Saturday, May 11, His thirty-first day in America, He rented one of the top story flats in the Hudson Apartment House, overlooking the Hudson River. As the friends joyously gathered to welcome Him back, He reviewed the trip:

It is only three weeks that we have been away from the New York friends, yet so great has been the longing to see you that it seems like three months. We have had no rest by day or night since we left you; either traveling, moving about or speaking; yet it was all so pleasantly done and we have been most happy. . . .
. . . We met savants and learned men and satisfied them with our explanations. . . .
Yesterday in Washington we met a group of important people. . . .
There were . . . at this meeting several cabinet officers, United States senators, many from the foreign diplomatic service, army and navy officials and other dignitaries. . . . We spoke to all from their own standpoints with most satisfactory results. . . .
In Washington, too, we called a meeting of the colored and white people. The attendance was very large,

the colored people predominating. At our second gathering this was reversed but at the third meeting we were unable to say which color predominated. These meetings were a great practical lesson upon the unity of colors and races in the Bahai teaching.[1]

On Sunday, May 12, the newspapers reported that Victor Herbert was offering the proceeds of a special concert to victims of the *Titanic*; that Grand Central Station was nearing completion; and that Mary Garden was giving a concert.

After prayer and tea 'Abdu'l-Bahá took the ferry to New Jersey and then caught a train for Montclair. The Reverend Edgar S. Wiers introduced Him to the congregation of Unity Church, saying:

> We need some great impelling message of peace. . . . class is set against class. The employer and the employee, the capitalist and wage earner confront each other with hatred. . . . Our own attitude of the white race toward the negro . . . and the red men . . . is anything but that which is indicated in our religion or any religion. . . . We need some great word that will bring us to . . . brotherhood, unity and love.
>
> . . . Just when we need the message of spiritual truth . . . this new religion has appeared. . . . One of the successions of men who has brought forward this religion—Abdul-Baha—will speak to us now. . . .[2]

After 'Abdu'l-Bahá spoke, He had lunch with some of the friends and seekers and with Mr. Wiers and his wife at the home of Charles Edsall; He then returned to New York in time to address the International Peace Forum.

On Monday, May 13, 'Abdu'l-Bahá was to appear at a meeting of the New York Peace Society. Juliet Thompson wrote, in an undated diary entry:

> The Master was really too ill to have gone to this Conference. He had been in bed all morning, suffering from complete exhaustion, and had a high temperature. I was with Him all morning. While I was sitting beside Him I asked: "*Must* You go to the Hotel Astor when You are so ill?" "I work by the confirmations of the Holy Spirit," He answered. "I do not work by hygienic laws. If I did," He laughed, "I would get nothing done."

The meeting of the Peace Society, held at the Hotel Astor, included preliminary comments by Rabbi Stephen S. Wise, Mrs. Anna Garland Spencer of the Ethical Society, the Reverend Percy Stickney Grant of the Church of the Ascension, Professor William Jackson of Columbia University, Mr. W. H. Short, secretary of the New York Peace Society, and Mr. Topakyan, Persian Consul General. In his remarks, Mr. Topakyan said, "Our guest of honor has stood as a Prophet of enlightenment and peace for the Persian Empire, and a well-wisher of Persia may well honor him," and concluded, "In closing I am happy to say that Abdul-Baha is the Glory of Persia today."[3]

He traveled the next day, Tuesday, May 14, to Lake Mohonk, the site of the International Peace Society's conference, to be the featured speaker of the evening. After the presentation the audience streamed to the platform to meet Him.

On May 15 'Abdu'l-Bahá walked around the beautiful grounds with a group of young people following Him. "'It is very easy,'" He told them, "'to come here, camp near this beautiful lake, on these charming hills, far away from everybody and deliver speeches on Universal Peace. These ideals should be spread and put in action over there, (Europe) not here in the world's most peaceful corner.'"[4]

May 15 was also a day for humor. The *Chicago Record-Herald* ran an article on May 14 which reported 'Abdu'l-Bahá's saying that this was the "all-right" nation, because that was the answer one received for almost any question.[5] The next day the catch phrase became the basis for an editorial in the same paper:

> Abdul Baha, the Persian prophet, thinks that the expression "All right" sums up the American character and spirit. These two magical words, he says, are not to be heard in any other country, while here they are on everybody's lips at all times. They reflect optimism, energy, go-aheadness. . . . Let sociologists dig and analyze, but for rough current speech the Persian prophet's observation is good enough. America *is* the All Right nation.

'Abdu'l-Bahá and His party stayed again overnight at Lake Mohonk, and on Thursday at about 9:00 P.M. an adventure began for Dr. Zia Bagdadi. 'Abdu'l-Bahá gave him the key to His New York apartment and asked him to get a Persian rug to give to Mr. Smiley, the president of the International Peace Society. Even though others said no one could make the journey and return before the scheduled departure at 10:00 A.M. the next morning, Dr. Bagdadi said, "I am not afraid to try anything for you, my Lord."

Since there were no passenger trains at that time of

night, Dr. Bagdadi jumped on the caboose of an already moving freight train. The trainman protested until he saw "Dr." written on the professional card and agreed to let the passenger remain on the train, not knowing his "urgent mission" concerned a rug. About 2:00 A.M. Dr. Bagdadi awakened Mrs. Grace Ober and her sister Ella Robarts, who were staying in 'Abdu'l-Bahá's apartment, selected a rug, dashed back to the station, caught a train, and arrived back at Lake Mohonk station with an hour left before 10:00 A.M. although an hour's drive lay ahead of him. The only vehicle in sight was the wagon of the mail carrier, who agreed to take him. Dr. Bagdadi arrived just as 'Abdu'l-Bahá was shaking hands with Mr. Smiley and preparing to leave. Mr. Smiley, on receiving the rug, said, "'Why this is just what I have been seeking for many years! You see, we had a Persian rug just like this one, but it was burned in a fire and ever since my wife has been broken-hearted over it. This will surely make her very happy.'"[6]

The secretary of the International Peace Society, in bidding 'Abdu'l-Bahá good-bye, said he was sorry religion could not be included in the organization, since its members included Protestants, Catholics, Jews, and others, and all would object if others were favored. 'Abdu'l-Bahá replied, "'Your members may be compared to beams of different metals and you are trying to unite them as you would tie these fingers together with a string. See, no matter how you tie them, still they remain separate. But the only way to make these metals into one alloy, is to put them into a crucible and apply intense heat to melt them all. For our melting-pot, we use the fire of the love of God.'"[7]

'Abdu'l-Bahá returned to New York City on Friday

afternoon, May 17, and told the waiting friends about the conference. On Saturday the talks and interviews continued all day long. Dr. Bagdadi recalled, ". . . He used to take a walk in the park along Riverside Drive. Often He went alone, and, knowing that the friends would like to accompany Him, He said, 'I sleep on the grass. I come out of fatigue. My mind rests. But when I am not alone, surely I talk, and rest of body and mind cannot be gained.'"[8]

'Abdu'l-Bahá spoke on Sunday morning, May 19, at the Church of the Divine Paternity, where Dr. Frank Hall, the minister, noted in his introduction that "this teaching has the power to bring together men of all classes. . . . to the Jew it sounds like Judaism; to the Christian, Christianity; to the Buddhist, Buddhism."[9]

In the evening He traveled to Jersey City and spoke in the Unitarian Church of which Howard Colby Ives was the pastor. Mr. Ives, in introducing 'Abdu'l-Bahá, said:

I hope I may be allowed to make one personal allusion. . . . There have come to this country vast numbers of so-called prophets,—people who came with a newism. . . . These Orientals line their pockets with our money and go away. . . . Lest you may think it is possible to believe such a thing of Abdul-Baha, let me tell you that his friends here provided a beautiful apartment for him in the Ansonia. . . . He accepted it with thanks, but paid for it all himself. Never since he has been in this country has he accepted one cent from anybody. On the contrary, the generosity of this noble soul is beyond any comparison. The first Sunday he spoke in Grant's church, the contribution was passed, and he made his offering. . . .

My friends, the Kingdom of God is at hand, and I call upon you to recognize it! I call upon you to spread the news on every side! . . .[10]

Monday and Tuesday were spent in interviews and public talks such as one to a Woman's Suffragist group in the Metropolitan Temple.

On Wednesday, May 22, 'Abdu'l-Bahá arrived in Boston and at 4:30 P.M. checked into the Hotel Charles where a large delegation greeted Him. He spoke at 8:00 P.M. that night to nearly three thousand persons, including eight hundred Unitarian ministers at the American Unitarian Association Conference. The presiding officer was the Lieutenant-Governor of Massachusetts, Robert Luce, who introduced Him to the audience, which gave Him a prolonged standing ovation. The headlines of the *Boston Evening Transcript* and the *Boston Evening Herald* the next morning read, "LARGEST IN YEARS: UNITARIAN FESTIVAL IN TREMONT TEMPLE ADDRESSED BY ORIENTAL SPEAKER," and "UNITARIANS RISE TO GREET PERSIAN SPEAKER AT TREMONT TEMPLE." 'Abdu'l-Bahá was described as being "Clad in shining raiment," and as making "a great impression on his listeners," who were referred to as "an attentive throng."

Great numbers of people flocked to see Him in Boston on Thursday, May 23. In the early afternoon He visited the Greek-Syrian Relief Society, where a reception featuring Eastern dishes was held. Before leaving He made a contribution to the agency. From there He drove with a university professor to Worcester. Along the way He commented on the greenness of the region and mentioned how much Bahá'u'lláh had enjoyed such scenes. Several times He asked the driver to stop, and the rest of the party stood and waited as He viewed the area.

At the University in Worcester He spoke to a special assembly including a thousand students and faculty members. The President provided Him with a car for traveling on to Cambridge to the home of Mrs. Francis W. Breed, where a large number of friends had gathered to celebrate 'Abdu'l-Bahá's sixty-eighth birthday. They brought out a cake with sixty-eight candles and miniature flags of the United States, Persia, and England adorning it. 'Abdu'l-Bahá lighted the first candle, and each of the friends lighted one in succession. 'Abdu'l-Baha proceeded to speak on the significance of that day as the time when the Báb declared His mission. The *Boston Evening Herald*, on May 26, in an article headed, "ABDUL BAHA IS BIRTHDAY GUEST," noted:

> There was a big birthday cake adorned with 68 tiny candles and three flags, the American flag in honor of the Boston Bahai Assembly, the Persian flag and the English flag, in honor of Miss Alice M. Buckston of England, author of "Eager Heart," and the daughter of the famous scientist. It was the wish of Abdul Baha to have the flag of every country on the cake, as he is universal, and considers every country his own, but there was not room for all. Abdul Baha made a short address at the conclusion of the feast.

On Friday, May 24, the inquirers and reporters visited Him until He went to Ford Hall in Boston and spoke to an audience of a thousand persons at the Free Religious Association of Unitarians. From there He drove to Brookline to speak and then back to the Boston hotel. Later He spoke for two hours at a meeting in the home of one of the friends.

The *Boston Traveler* that day included an article headed "Abdul Baha Has Creed He Declares Will Finally Eliminate Criminals." It reported His saying, "'No, I do not believe in capital punishment. . . . If the Bahai movement is widely successful it will hold such sway over the moral, intellectual and physical character of the race that there will not be a criminal to be found.'"

On Saturday, May 25, after a day of individual interviews, He went to a farewell dinner at Huntington Chambers Hall and spoke to an audience of a thousand people.

On Sunday morning, May 26, 'Abdu'l-Bahá prepared to return to New York for yet another visit. The *New York World* recorded such events as the death of the sister of Leo Tolstoy and a walking trip of Upton Sinclair. The *New York Herald* wrote of a memorial being planned to Lincoln in an article headed, "'Why a Greek Colonnade to Lincoln,' Ask American Architects?" The *New York Times* reported that a commission would study pellagra and that, in Tyler, Texas, "Two Thousand Aid in Burning Negro at the Stake."

Before leaving Boston at noon 'Abdu'l-Bahá visited a Syrian organization. He reached New York at 6:00 P.M., stopped at the Edward B. Kinney home, and then went to the Mount Morris Baptist Church, where the minister, J. Herman Randall, introduced Him. 'Abdu'l-Bahá told them:

the words I speak to you here tonight may produce no effect whatever. Some hearts may be affected, then

soon forget; others owing to superstitious ideas and
imaginations may even fail to hear and understand, but
the blessed souls who are attentive to my exhortation
and admonition, listening with the ear of acceptance,
allowing my words to penetrate effectively will advance
day by day toward full fruition. . . .[11]

On Tuesday, May 28, 'Abdu'l-Bahá was evicted from
His hotel because, as Maḥmúd noted, of the "coming and
going of diverse people" and the "additional labors and
troubles" for the staff and the "incessant inquiries" directed to the hotel management. "But," Maḥmúd continued, "when the people of the hotel saw His great kindness and favor at the time of His departure, they were
ashamed of their conduct and begged Him to stay longer,
but He would not accept." He moved to Saffa Kinney's
home at 780 West End Avenue.

On the same day 'Abdu'l-Bahá was the principal
speaker at one of the peace forums popular just before the
First World War. It was held at the Metropolitan Temple
and drew an audience of one thousand. He was introduced by the Reverend Frederick Lynch who had met
Him before: "It may interest you to know where I first saw
him. It was at Charles Grant Kennedy's play, the 'Terrible Meek.' . . . I had the pleasure next of seeing him at
Lake Mohonk and hearing the most remarkable address I
have ever listened to. . . ."[12]

The *New York City American*, the next day, in an article
headed, "URGES ONE RELIGION FOR ALL," reported about the meeting:

The Metropolitan Temple was filled yesterday with
a fashionable and distinguished audience greeting

Abdul Baha Abbas. Upon the platform were seated the Rev. Wesley J. Hill, former pastor of the Metropolitan Templ., Church, who presided; the Rev. Rabbi Silverman and the Rev. Dr. Frederick Lynch, all of whom spoke. . . .

Abdul Baha said that divine religions, like the waters, are in reality one. He advocated one universal religion with no racial difference.

On Thursday, May 30, as Ethel Barrymore announced her intention to play in vaudeville, and the bubonic plague broke out in Hong Kong, 'Abdu'l-Bahá spoke at the Theosophical Lodge and at the University of New York.

On Friday the papers announced a waiters' strike and the death of Wilbur Wright of typhoid fever and stated that future physicians would be hypnotists and psychologists. 'Abdu'l-Bahá went to Fanwood, New Jersey, where He visited Hoar's Sanitorium, conducted a morning public meeting, and presented an afternoon address in the Town Hall. The friends entreated Him to stay in the refreshing country air for a few days; but He replied, "'We have no time for amusement. We must engage ourselves in the service of the Threshold of God.'"

On Saturday, June 1, the *New York Times* reported a "color line" at the University of Michigan, which banned Hindu students. 'Abdu'l-Bahá went to the train station accompanied by weeping friends and returned to New York where He told the friends about the Fanwood trip.

One of the inquirers that afternoon was a Socialist, to whom 'Abdu'l-Bahá said:

Go to the *socialists* and say that partnership in the properties and lands of this world is the source of strife

and warfare. But partnership and inheritance in the
Kingdom are a cause of love and amity. If you will put
your efforts to gain the precepts of the Kingdom instead
of worldly rights, you will gain perpetual happiness.

Maḥmúd noted: "Every person with a particular interest
was addressed similarly."

7

Magazine Accounts

Beginning in June virtually every major magazine in the country and scores of smaller ones wrote of 'Abdu'l-Bahá, interviewed Him, or editorialized about Him. *The American Review of Reviews*, in its June issue, summed up several other accounts in an article entitled "Will Bahaism Unite All Religious Faiths?"

"Surely the dawn of a new day was heralded on that Sunday evening when the Archdeacon of Westminster walked hand in hand with the venerable Abdul Baha up the nave of St. John's Church [London], and invited him not only to address the congregation but to offer for them his prayers and blessing," says a writer in the *Fortnightly Review*.
Considering the dignity and conservatism of the Established Church of England, and the fact that this little-known Persian prophet has come to the western world to proclaim the dawn of the millenium, to announce that the Messiah awaited by all nations has actually lived, taught and died upon this earth within the past century, and to preach what he and his followers believe to be the new world religion, designed to include and supersede all others and to unite all nations

under the banner of a common faith, this would hardly seem an extravagant statement. When we add to it the assertion of the *Contemporary Review* that, within a week after his arrival in England, where he was almost unknown, Abdul Baha delivered an address from the pulpit of the City Temple in London, being introduced by its rector as the leader of one of the most remarkable religious movements of this or any other age, it seems evident that at least a part of the Episcopal Church is inclined to accord him the courtesy of a respectful hearing.

Religionists of other faiths were equally interested. The *Fortnightly Review* goes on to say:

> To the house in London [Lady Blomfield's house] where Abdul Baha and his suite were received as honored, welcome guests, came a constant stream of all sorts and conditions of men and women, Christians of every denomination, Buddhists of every nationality, Theosophists, Zoroastrians and Mohammedans, Agnostics and Gnostics. To each he spoke some individual message, and to their varied questions he gave simple, direct and quite spontaneous answers.

> A few weeks ago Abdul Baha and his little group of disciples landed in New York, quietly and almost unheralded by the newspapers. Courtesies similar to those he had received in London were at once extended to him by the Rev. Percy Stickney Grant and others of the clergy. . . . he has been speaking constantly to those who cared to seek him out. . . .

> Abdul Baha . . . makes no claim that he is himself

the Messiah. He says plainly that he is not even a prophet, only Abdul Baha, the servant of God. But he and his followers believe and assert that the Messiah expected by all peoples came in the form of Baha'u'llah, who spent the greater part of his life a prisoner in the Syrian penal colony at Acca, and who died there fourteen years ago. . . .

The absolute catholicity of the doctrine goes far toward explaining its ready acceptance by adherents of every known creed. . . . The Bahai who is not made thereby a better Christian, Mohammedan or Buddhist, is no true Bahai. . . .

There is something above and beyond patriotism, and it is better to love your fellowmen than to love only your countrymen. When we see this, and know in very truth the brotherhood of man, war will appear to us in its true light as an outrage on civilization, an act of madness and blindness. The sole point is that the fundamentals of spiritual teaching shall be universally admitted and practically applied to the affairs of daily life and to the development of the social and political life of nations. . . .

Baha'u'llah announced this half a century ago, in the slaughter-house of Persia, and it is not less forcible because to-day it is the slogan of Peace Societies in every civilized country in the world. So with other ideals which men are striving to realize. They all form integral parts of the teachings of Baha'u'llah. . . .

Abdul Baha lays great stress upon the necessity of a vital and burning faith, says the *Fortnightly Review*, but he has little use for faith without works. Numerous instances are given of questions asked by members of different cults, and his replies, far from encouraging a more or less unproductive mysticism, urged the necessity of proving the value of every theory by practical application. On the other hand, practical, in the sense he used it, does not in the least mean profitable. One of the most rigid rules of Bahaism is that no religious teacher shall receive a salary, or payment of any kind, for giving forth the truth as he has received it, but shall support himself and his family by the work of his hands or the practice of some profession. . . .[1]

In its June issue the magazine *Current Literature* included, together with a full page of photographs, an article headed "The Universal Gospel That Abdul Baha Brings Us":

Toward the end of April there landed in New York an old man with a white turban and flowing beard, clad in strange garments and speaking a strange tongue. Hundreds welcomed him at the dock, and thousands have attended his receptions and public addresses in many American cities. He is Abdul Baha, "Servant of the Glory," head of the Bahaist movement, and one of the most distinguished religious figures of the age.

Those who have met him bear witness to his loving kindness, to his spiritual breadth, and to his physical frailty. For forty years he was imprisoned in Persia. His father, Baha Ullah, died in prison. The Bab, the founder of the Bahaist faith, was executed, and so were thousands of his followers. It is only during recent years, since the young Turks came into possession of the government and gave Persia a constitution, that Abdul Baha has been free to travel.

He visited London first and received a warm welcome there. The Rev. R. J. Campbell and Archdeacon Wilberforce offered him their pulpits for the exploitation of his views. Now he has come to America to get into personal touch with followers and friends. A new group of buildings for worship, for healing and for education is being erected in his honor in Chicago. His first public appearance in this country was in the Church of the Ascension, New York, where the Rev. Dr. Percy Stickney Grant introduced him with the words: "He teaches the fundamental unity of all religions. . . ."

. . . In the Bible of the City Temple, London, he wrote: "This book is the Holy Book of God, of celestial inspiration." In the same spirit he would write the same words upon the Koran or the Vedas.

Bahaism recognizes not only the Bibles of the world but also its different saviors and prophets. Jesus, Mohammed, Buddha . . . Baha Ullah—all were necessary in their time and place. The supreme need of the hour, as Abdul Baha sees it, is a deeper unity. He teaches the substitution of arbitration for war. . . . He believes in monogamic marriage, in woman suffrage and in a universal language. . . . When asked by a New York *Times* reporter to formulate his message to America, he said:

"The time has arrived for the world of humanity to hoist the standard of the oneness of the human world, so that solidarity and unity may connect all the nations of the world, so that dogmatic formulas and superstitions may end, so that the essential reality underlying all the religions founded by all the prophets may be revealed.

"That reality is one.

"It is the love of God.

"It is the progress of the world.

"It is the oneness of humanity.

"It is the bond which can unite all the human race.

"It is the attainment of the benefits of the most great peace; it is the discarding of warfare.

"It is progressiveness; it is the undertaking of co-lossal tasks in life; it is the oneness of public opinion.

"Therefore strive, oh ye people, and put forth your efforts that this reality may overcome the lesser forces in life, that this king of reality may alone rule all humanity.

"Thus may the world of mankind be reformed.

"Thus may a new Springtime be ushered in and a fresh spirit may resuscitate man.

"The individuals of humanity, like refreshed plants, shall put forth leaves and shall blossom and fructify so that the face of the earth shall become the long promised and delectable paradise, so that the great bestowal—the supreme virtues of man—shall glisten over the face of the earth.

"Then shall the world of existence have attained maturity.

"This is my message."

The universal gospel of Bahaism finds fruitful soil in America, and is greeted sympathetically in both secular and religious papers. "No religious movement of recent

times," in the judgment of the Portland *Oregonian* "is
nearly so significant as that of Bahaism." The Boston
Congregationalist declares: "The religion of the Bahaists
has nothing of the eccentricity or faddism of so many
modern religions and none of their shallow philosophy. . . .

The New York *Churchman*, however, registers an
objection against the appearance of Abdul Baha in
Christian pulpits:

> ". . . Its [the Bahá'í Faith's] purpose is, no doubt,
> laudable; and it excites the sympathy of those who
> see in all the great ethnic religions glimpses of that
> Light which lighteth every man that cometh into the
> world.
>
> "But Bahaism is not Christianity; and Abdul Baha
> does not profess to be a Christian. What right, then,
> has he to preach in a Christian church?"

In much stronger language the Philadelphia
Presbyterian expresses its distrust of the whole Bahaist
movement, which it describes as "pantheistic." The
Chicago *Advance* also comments caustically: "Bahaism
may be summed up in the word that 'nothing matters.'
All religions are equally true or equally false, as you
may choose to put it. It seems to have but one article in
its creed and that is 'universal tolerance.' As a civil creed
that is sound. As an ethical creed that is rotten."

But as long as the watchwords of Bahaism are Universal Peace, Universal Education, Universal Brotherhood, its influence, a writer in *The Christian Register*
thinks, need not be feared. "Rather," he says, "should it
be welcomed as one more indication of the drawing

together of races and the coming cooperation of man in the establishment of what in both Eastern and Western language is called the Kingdom of God." Francis Henry Skrine, the author of a new book on Bahaism (published by Longmans, Green & Company), finds the new cult suited to the present American mood of revolt against materialism and predatory wealth. "Bahaism," he says, "may come in the great republic with a rush which nothing can resist."[2]

8

New York, Philadelphia, New York

On Sunday, June 2, the *New York Times* announced, in a special report from Montclair, New Jersey, "BAHA TO LIVE IN MONTCLAIR. FAMOUS PERSIAN RELIGIOUS LEADER TAKES A HOUSE THERE." The report continued:

> Abdul Baha, . . . head of the Bahaists, who number 14,000,000 throughout the world, will make his home in Montclair. The Persian prophet . . . has taken the house at 11 Bradford Place . . . and will live there after June 15.
> Abdul Baha recently spoke in Unity Church here, and was so impressed by the reception he received and by the physical aspects of the town that he expressed a desire to take up his abode in the town. . . .

Other events were also reported: the population of the United States had risen above 100,000,000; and Nijinsky's dancing in Debussey's "daring" ballet *Afternoon of a Faun* had stirred the Paris critics.

'Abdu'l-Bahá returned to the Church of the Ascension that evening, and, after a brief talk, answered questions submitted on slips of paper from the audience:

Question: What relation do you sustain to the founder of your belief? Are you his successor in the same manner as the Pope of Rome?

Answer: I am the servant of Baha 'Ullah the founder and in this I glory. No honor do I consider greater than this. . . .

Question: What is the relation of the Bahai teaching to the ancient Zoroastrian religion?

Answer: The religions of God have the same foundation but the dogmas appearing later have differed. Each of the divine religions has two aspects. The first is essential. It concerns morality and development of the virtues of the human world. This aspect is common to all. . . . The second aspect of the divine religions is non-essential. It concerns human needs and undergoes change in every cycle according to the exigency of the time. . . .

Question: Is peace a greater word than love?

Answer: No! love is greater than peace, for peace is founded upon love. . . . Until love is attained, peace cannot be. . . .

Question: Will women or men aid this new religion most?

Answer: In Persia the men have aided it more but in the west perchance the women.[1]

Among 'Abdu'l-Bahá's visitors on Monday morning, June 3, was the actor Walter Hampden, who was playing the part of Jesus in *The Servant in the House*. He came every day thereafter until 'Abdu'l-Bahá left for New Hampshire. Another visitor was a cabinet member who invited 'Abdu'l-Bahá to visit his estate outside the city. There, as Maḥmúd noted, "For one day and night the statesmen and notables of the Republic were immersed in a state of rapture and fascinated at seeing the world illuminating Face." He further noted that "a resume of all the addresses and the detailed answers to questions which He made during that one day and night" would be in themselves "a detailed book."

On Tuesday, June 4, before leaving the estate, 'Abdu'l-Bahá called all the servants together and gave each of them money. On His return to New York, 'Abdu'l-Bahá went to the house He had rented along the Hudson River.

The newspapers reported a "wave of revolt" over Belgium and an internal "war" in Cuba against rebels. 'Abdu'l-Bahá went to the Unity Club on Wednesday to speak to a children's affair at which various civic leaders and statesmen, and Admiral Peary, were also present. He spoke that evening at the Women's Union on the education of women.

On Thursday, June 6, one newspaper carried an article headed "Tracing Darrow Fund," which described how the lawyer, Clarence Darrow, had been accused of jury bribing. 'Abdu'l-Bahá, in addition to speaking with the scores of people who surged to His home, took time for a ride in a public park in Brooklyn and a walk alone in the little garden near His home. The next day, Maḥmúd noted, "One of the servants showed such negligence and impudence that the Most Holy Heart and the hearts of the servants of the Holy Threshold were made sad."

On Saturday, June 8, the *Philadelphia Inquirer* carried this notation in the "Week's Religious News," under "Unitarian": "Abdul Baha, the Persian exile and centre of the Bahai movement, who speaks at the Girard Avenue Unitarian Church tomorrow morning, has had a most interesting history. . . . Even through an interpreter he is an elegant speaker." Other headlines read: "Gangsters Again Engaged in a Murderous War"; "Foreign and American Colleges to Exchange Students"; "Ty Cobb a Merchant: Detroit's Famous Ballplayer Busy at Interest in a Sporting Goods Firm"; and "Rush Warships to Havana."

'Abdu'l-Bahá arrived in Philadelphia at 6:00 P.M. that same day and went to the Hotel Rittenhouse. Maḥmúd wrote, "He was in a very exhausted . . . state. Notwithstanding this, He made two speeches before the friends. . . . On account of excessive exhaustion, He did not attend some of the meetings and tendered His apology."

On Sunday morning, June 9, He drove to 15th Street and Girard Avenue where the Unitarian Church was located and told the congregation of some of the major Teachings of Bahá'u'lláh. In the afternoon He received visitors, including reporters, who came to His hotel rooms. That evening He spoke before the congregation of twenty-five hundred in the Baptist Temple, at Broad and Berks streets. In His lengthy address He elaborated on nine of the principles of the Bahá'í Faith.

At 9:30 A.M., Monday, June 10, He addressed a group of fifty people at the home of Jesse Revell. Until His train left at 3:00 P.M. for New York, He conducted interviews at the Revells' and at the Hotel Rittenhouse.

Back in New York for a ten-day visit 'Abdu'l-Bahá continued to see streams of people who lined up day and night for interviews. On June 11 He spoke with the friends several times and, at one session, told them of His recent trip:

We have just returned from a visit to Philadelphia. . . . Sometimes the difficulties are arduous
but out of love for the friends of God and with desire
to sacrifice myself in the pathway of God, I bear them
in gladness. The purpose is the result which is accomplished, love and unity among mankind. For the world
is dark with discord and selfishness, hearts are negli-
gent, souls are bereft of God. . . . Man is submerged in
the affairs of this world. . . . Desire and passion like
two unmanageable horses have wrested the reins of control from him and are galloping madly in the wilder-
ness. . . .

I have come to this country in the advanced years of
my life, undergoing difficulties of health and climate
because of excessive love for the friends of God. . . .
For service in love for mankind is unity with God. . . .[2]

About that hectic Tuesday, Juliet Thompson wrote on
June 12:

. . . Yesterday morning I went up early to the
Master's house—that house whose door is open at
seven-thirty and kept wide open till midnight. . . .

. . . He talked for a long while to the people. But this
I could see was pure sacrifice. His vitality seemed *gone*.
At times He could scarcely bring forth the words, yet
He gave and gave. When He had finished He hurriedly
left the house and went again to "His Garden." On the
way to the bus I met Him returning alone.

He stopped me, put out His hand and took mine,
with indescribable tenderness smiling at me.

"That night," Juliet continued, "there was a meeting at the Kinneys'—one of those deadly 'Board meetings'—but the Master came to it. Striding up and down like a king, He spoke to us." Howard MacNutt recorded His words:

> It is my hope that the meetings of the Bahai Assembly in New York shall become like meetings of the Supreme Concourse. . . . In discussions look toward the reality without being self-opinionated. Let no one assert and insist upon his own mere opinion; nay, rather, let each investigate the reality with the greatest love and fellowship. Consult upon every matter and when one presents the point of view of the reality itself, that shall be acceptable to all. Then will spiritual unity increase among you, individual illumination will be greater, happiness more abundant and you will draw nearer and nearer to the Kingdom of God.[3]

On June 13 the continuing streams of people prompted 'Abdu'l-Bahá to instruct those with Him, "'If anyone who has not seen Me as yet wishes to see Me, or if anyone has some urgent business, inform Me. All others I will meet in the public meeting, because I have neither time nor strength to see people individually.'"

On Sunday morning, June 16, a sign stood in front of the Fourth Unitarian Church on Beverly Road in Flatbush, proclaiming, "'The Great Persian Prophet, His Holiness Abdul Baha Will Speak in this Church at 11:00 A.M. on the 16th of June.'" When 'Abdu'l-Bahá ended His talk and the service concluded, the excited congregation came to greet and thank Him. The minister asked Him to visit the children in the Sunday School. They gathered about Him, and He said, "Praise be to God! I see before me these beautiful children of the kingdom."[4]

After lunch at Mr. MacNutt's home He spoke to large numbers of the friends until time to go to an evening meeting at the Central Congregational Church on Hancock Street in Brooklyn. Before an audience that received Him eagerly 'Abdu'l-Bahá delivered from the Christian pulpit one of His lengthiest addresses, demonstrating with great force the proofs of the Prophethood of Muḥammad and Bahá'u'lláh.

One newspaper on Monday morning, June 17, noted that "Helen Keller Would Be Socialist Orator: Deaf-Blind Wonder to Train for Career in Schenectady Welfare Board" and that "Plans for Celebrating a Safe and Sane Fourth of July Underway." In discussing the meeting held the previous evening, 'Abdu'l-Bahá said, "'I established the Truth of Islám in the great churches in this way. What have the Muḥammadans now to say about us?'"

Then a writer for a national magazine visited Him, asking for detailed material on the Teachings of the Bahá'í Faith. Later that day Maḥmúd noted, "In these days, He often commanded the friends to teach the Cause of God and to travel in the neighboring countries. 'They must teach the Cause of God,' He said, 'with great meekness and humility.'" To the group of friends who assembled He spoke of the dire necessity of reading the Writings of Bahá'u'lláh, likening them to the prescription of the Divine Physician.

Tuesday was the day of movie-making. Previously, a motion-picture company had filmed 'Abdu'l-Bahá at the entrance of the Hotel Ansonia for national distribution. This gave the Bahá'ís the idea of making a more extensive film. On June 18, at the home of Mr. MacNutt, five different sequences were photographed. After that Maḥmúd noted, "He went to see a Jewish friend who was ill at his home, which was forty miles from Brooklyn. He returned exhausted at night to New York."

On Wednesday, June 19, Juliet Thompson was finishing her portrait of 'Abdu'l-Bahá, while Lua Getsinger sat nearby on the couch. Juliet recalled:

> He sat still as a statue, His eyes closed, infinite peace on that chisled face, a God-like calm and grandeur in His erect head.
>
> Suddenly—with a great flash—like lightening—He opened His eyes and the room seemed to rock like a ship in a storm with the Power released. The Master was *blazing*. "The veils of glory"—"the thousand veils" —had shriveled away in that Flame and we were exposed to the Glory Itself. . . .
>
> Then He spoke to Lua. . . .
>
> "I appoint you, Lua, the Herald of the Covenant. And I AM THE COVENANT, appointed by Bahá'u'lláh. And no one can refute His Word. This is the Testament of Bahá'u'lláh. You will find it in the Holy Book of Aqdas. Go forth and proclaim, 'This is THE COVENANT OF GOD in your midst.'"
>
> "Oh, re-create me," she cried, "that I may do this work for Thee!"

Shortly afterward He sent Mrs. Getsinger downstairs to the waiting believers to "proclaim the Covenant." Then 'Abdu'l-Bahá Himself went down to speak.

To underline His dynamic explanations of the Covenant 'Abdu'l-Bahá had the Tablet of the Branch translated and read to the entire body. The believers, crowding into the room and sitting on the stairs, listened to the words written by Bahá'u'lláh: "Whosoever turns to Him hath surely turned unto God, and whosoever turneth away from Him hath turned away from My beauty, denied My proof and is of those who transgress."[5] 'Abdu'l-Bahá also designated New York as the "City of the Covenant."

As 'Abdu'l-Bahá prepared to leave New York for a few days, the book, *The Brilliant Proof*, written by Mírzá Abu'l-Faḍl in answer to a London minister's criticism of the Cause, arrived. 'Abdu'l-Bahá was pleased with the work and ordered it to be translated and printed.[6]

Later that Wednesday, when some of the friends described places for sightseeing in America, 'Abdu'l-Bahá remarked, "'We love meetings of fidelity and not picturesque scenes. We must first be faithful to God, to His laws and Covenant and then to His servants. If we wish to see places of interest and picturesque scenes we should do so when we go to pay visits or when we have to pass through such places and scenes.'"

On Thursday, June 20, Juliet Thompson wrote (in a diary entry dated July 5):

> . . . we went to Mrs. Kasebier's—Lua, Mrs. Hinkle-Smith, and I—in the car with the Master.
>
> I shall never forget the Master's beauty in the strange cold light of her studio—a green, *under-water* sort of light, in which He looked shining and chisled—like the statue of a god.

Of that afternoon and the succession of people who came and asked questions of 'Abdu'l-Bahá, Maḥmúd recalled these experiences:

Mrs. Smith, a member of one of the distinguished families of Philadelphia, had recently embraced the cause and requested a Persian name. She was given the name of Tábanda. Prescribing some medicine for her headache, He said, "You must be happy always. You must be counted among the people of joy and happiness and must be adorned with divine morals. In a large measure happiness keeps our health while depression of spirit begets diseases. The substance of eternal happiness is spirituality and divine morality, which has no sorrow to follow it. Physical happiness is subject to a thousand changes and vicissitudes. . . ."

Another friend asked about trials and unexpected troubles.

He replied, "Creation is interwoven in a natural law and divine order. Everything is interlinked. A link cannot be broken without its having something to do with that natural order. . . ."

Philosophical explanations and solutions of intricate problems issued forth from the Holy lips in every gathering, while the minds of the hearers were recipients of eternal bounties.

Before leaving New York, 'Abdu'l-Bahá issued an invitation to a gathering of the friends:

I am about to leave the city for a few days rest at Montclair. When I return it is my wish to give a large feast of unity. A place for it has not yet been found. It must be outdoors under the trees, in some location away from city noise; like a Persian garden. The food will be Persian food. When the place is arranged all will be informed and we will have a general meeting in which hearts will be bound together, spirits blended and a new foundation for unity established. All the friends will come. They will be my guests. . . .[7]

9

New Jersey:
The Unity Feast

'Abdu'l-Bahá arrived in Montclair, New Jersey, on Friday, June 21, staying in a house He had rented in advance. Most of His time was occupied in talking with the people who came to see Him. On Sunday morning, June 23, 'Abdu'l-Bahá told the Bahá'ís more of the history of the Faith. As He came into the living room where the people were gathered, He said to one of the incoming friends, "You are always smiling." Mr. Frank E. Osborne replied, "Surely our faces should reflect happiness in this presence." 'Abdu'l-Bahá replied, "Yes!—This is the day of Baha' Ullah; the age of the Blessed Perfection; the cycle of the Greatest Name. If you do not smile now, for what time will you await and what greater happiness could you expect?"[1]

That same day Juliet Thompson and Lua Getsinger brought the proofs of Mrs. Kasebier's photographs for the Master to see. They were sitting on the closed-in front porch in the afternoon with a number of the friends. Juliet recalled, in an undated entry in her diary:

I showed Him the proofs of the pictures, then spoke of Mrs. Kasebier—who had seen Him only once, when she photographed Him.

"She said she would like to live near You, my Lord."

He laughed. "She doesn't want to live near Me. She only wants a good time!" Then He grew serious. "To live near Me," He said, "one must have My aims and objects. Do you remember the rich young man who wanted to live near Christ, and when he learned what *it cost* to live near Him—that it meant to give away all his possessions and take up a cross and follow Christ —then," the Master laughed, "he *fled away*!"

"Among the disciples of the Báb," He continued, "were two: His amanuensis and a firm believer. On the eve of the Báb's martyrdom the firm believer prayed, 'Oh let me die with You!' The amanuensis said: 'What shall I do?'

"'What shall I do,'" mocked the Master. "'What do you want me to do?' The disciple died with the Báb, his head on the breast of the Báb, and their bodies were mingled in death. The other died in prison anyway, but think of the difference in their stations!"

"There was another martyr," continued the Master after a moment, "Mírzá Abdu'lláh of Shíráz." Then He told us that Mírzá Abdu'lláh had been in the Presence of Bahá'u'lláh only once, "But he so loved the Blessed Beauty" that he *could not resist* following Him to Ṭihrán. . . .

Mírzá Abdu'lláh reached Ṭihrán in the midst of that bloodiest of massacres. . . . Bahá'u'lláh had been cast into a dungeon. There, in that foul cellar He sat, weighted down by "The Devil's Chain"—eleven disciples sitting with Him, bound by the same chain. In it were set iron collars which were fastened around the neck by iron pins. Every day a disciple was slaughtered and none knew when his turn would come. The first intimation he had of his immediate death was when the jailer took out the iron pin from his collar.

Mírzá Abdu'lláh entered Ṭihrán and inquired of the guard at the gate "where Bahá'u'lláh resided." "We will take you to Him," said the guard. And some men took Abdu'lláh to the dungeon and chained him to Bahá'u'lláh.

"So," the Master said, "he found his Beloved again!"

One day the jailer came into the dungeon and took the pin from Mírzá Abdu'lláh's collar.

"Then," said the Master, "Mírzá Abdu'lláh stepped joyfully forward. First, he kissed the feet of the Blessed Beauty—and then—"

The Master's whole aspect suddenly changed. It was as though the spirit of the martyr had entered into Him. With that God-like head erect, snapping His fingers high in the air, beating out a drum-like rhythm with His foot—till we could hardly endure the vibrations set up, He triumphantly sang "The Martyr's Song."

> "I have come again, I have come again,
> By way of <u>Sh</u>íráz I have come again!
> With the wine-cup in My hand!
> Such is the madness of Love!"

"And thus," ended 'Abdu'l-Bahá, "singing and dancing he went to his death—and a hundred executioners fell on him! And later his parents came to Bahá'u'lláh, praising God that their son had given his life in the Path of God." . . .

The Master sank back into His chair. Tears swelled

in my eyes, blurring everything. . . . A smile of exultation played on His lips. So low that it sounded like an echo He hummed the Martyr's Song.

The rest of the week 'Abdu'l-Bahá spent in instructing the friends and visitors who flocked to His doors in Montclair and in making a brief trip to Newark. After early morning prayers 'Abdu'l-Bahá usually went to the market Himself to purchase food for the day; He managed most of the meals Himself, especially if guests were present, as there usually were.

After He breakfasted at Mr. Charles Edsall's home on Wednesday, June 26, and returned to His house, He found several of the ladies who had come down from New York hard at work washing dishes and cleaning floors. 'Abdu'l-Bahá laughed and said, "'Look! How the power of the Blessed Beauty works!'"

In Newark, on Thursday, as they walked through the park, the Persian friends were aware of passersby staring at the unusual scene of the American friends following in reverence after 'Abdu'l-Bahá. On Friday, when He took a group of the friends by streetcar to the park in Montclair, He led them to the empty bandstand, and seated them saying, "'factious persons . . . are trying to imprison Me again on My return to the Holy Land.'" When the friends suggested it would be better for Him not to return, He replied, "'My source is the Holy Threshold. What I have is from that Threshold, and my return, too, is to the same. Had it not been for His aid and assistance, would these people sitting on your right and left have had any care for you and Me? . . . What are we and why are we showered with these favors? Where is Persia and where is America? . . .'"

Visiting Mr. Topakyan,
the Persian Consul General,
Morristown, New Jersey, June 30, 1912

'Abdu'l-Bahá at the Unity Feast,
West Englewood, New Jersey, June 29, 1912

'Abdu'l-Bahá with a Small Group of Bahá'ís,
West Englewood, New Jersey, June 29, 1912

He then walked to a nearby hotel, and two ladies, seeing Him, asked to be introduced and proceeded to ask Him about the history and teachings of the Faith. When they said that He seemed to be extremely wealthy, He responded, "'My riches are of the Kingdom and not of this world. . . . Although I have nothing, yet I am richer than all the world.'" A couple passing by stopped to listen and joined the conversation. They gave their names to Mr. Edsall so they could be invited to meetings.

Maḥmúd noted, that day, "He ['Abdu'l-Bahá] used to say, 'Had I sufficient rest and repose and a little relaxation of thought you would have seen how the hearts would have been attracted and the souls set aglow.'"

It was not, however, His talks on spiritual development that found their way into the *New York Times* on Sunday. In an article headed, "PROPHET'S DASH FOR TRAIN: Abdul Baha in Spectacular Rush from Montclair," the *Times* reported:

> Special to the New York Times / Montclair, N.J. June 29—The departure of Abdul Baha, leader of the Bahaist cult, from Montclair to-day was attended by excitement. Abdul Baha and a retinue of ten fez-wearing Persians had been staying at 11 Bradford Place for several weeks. Arrangements were made for the departure of the aged prophet to-day for West Englewood. . . . Several members of his retinue left for the Lackawanna station in advance of their leader.
>
> When train time came, Abdul Baha was not in sight. He had been delayed. The baggage of the Persians was aboard the train, and as it moved away they appealed to the trainmen in several Oriental languages to defer the departure for a few minutes. Several of the excited

followers of the prophet, when they realized that the train was leaving, jumped to the platforms. One of them, in swinging his arms about, accidently or otherwise, pulled the bell rope. At the same instant, by a strange coincidence, Abdul Baha hove in sight in an automobile. To add to the excitement a Persian accidentally knocked off the conductor's hat. The train came to a halt, and Abdul Baha leaped from the automobile and was hustled aboard the coach by his friends.

'Abdu'l-Bahá left Montclair at 8:30 A.M. on Saturday, June 29, and, after transfering to four different streetcars, arrived at Roy Wilhelm's home in West Englewood, New Jersey. This was the large outdoor gathering—the Unity Feast—to which 'Abdu'l-Bahá had invited the friends before He left New York. He rested as the friends arrived and sat in a circle in the shade of the large trees. Then He spoke to individuals as He walked among them. Addressing the entire group He said, "This is a new Day and this hour is a new Hour in which we have come together. . . . True Bahai meetings are the mirrors of the kingdom wherein images of the Supreme Concourse are reflected. . . . First, you must become united and agreed among yourselves. . . ."[2]

When He had finished, the meal was ready; but just as it was announced, thunder was heard, and large raindrops began to fall. 'Abdu'l-Bahá walked to the road, taking a chair, and several friends grouped around Him. As He sat, His face turned upward, a strong wind began to blow, the clouds began to disperse, and the sun shown through. Then He rose and walked back into the grove. After the meal of Persian food 'Abdu'l-Bahá annointed the two hundred fifty guests with attar of roses. After dark, as the friends sat on the lawn with candles, 'Abdu'l-Bahá spoke, ending as He walked into the darkness, "Peace be with you. I will pray for you."[3]

On Sunday morning, June 30, 'Abdu'l-Bahá left for the home of Mr. Topakyan, the Persian Consul General, in Morristown. On His way there He stopped in Englewood at the home of the minister who had come to see Him the day before. After talking a few minutes, He continued His trip to Morristown. Concerning the afternoon activities, 'Abdu'l-Bahá's translator, Dr. Amín Faríd, wrote:

> The Consul-General of Persia, Topakyan, gave a barbecue in honor of Abdul-Baha and his Persian suite, at his delightful summer home and garden at Morristown, New Jersey. The journey was accomplished in an automobile from the home of Mr. Roy C. Wilhelm, in West Englewood, through beautiful meadows of New Jersey, and the whole day was spent most pleasantly at the Persian consulate, which is a building in the garden built after the old style of Persian architecture. Among the guests were some prominent men from New York and some society folk to interview him on all sorts of questions. He spoke that forenoon to those persons on the advance of materialism and its evil attendants or concomitants. The dinner was entirely Oriental in character, a barbecue a la Perse.[4]

On returning to New York that night, Maḥmúd recalled, "the Blessed One did not allow us to prepare supper. After partaking of a little bread and watermelon, He went to bed."

10

New York City

On July 1 'Abdu'l-Bahá had been in America for eighty-one days. When the July issue of *Hearst's Magazine* appeared on the stands, it included Elbert Hubbard's article, "A Modern Prophet," in which he said:

['Abdu'l-Bahá] has diverted one-third of the population of Persia from Mohammedanism. Throughout all Asia, Europe and the United States, there are constantly growing bodies of adherents to the faith of Abdul Baha.

This man comes to the Western world on a distinct mission, and no one who meets him can doubt his sincerity. He is no mere eccentric.

The message he brings is the unification of the East and West in the bonds of brotherly love, mutual aid, reciprocity and an understanding which means peace on earth and good will toward men.

It presages a world-wide up-swinging of vital religion. . . .

One distinguishable and peculiar thing about Abdul Baha is that he does not make war upon, or even criticize, any other religious faith. . . .

. . . he was in prison. But even his jailers dared not forbid him sending out his messages of faith.

Even in prison he was treated with a reverence and awe that is not very difficult to understand when you meet the man.

Abdul Baha is a most remarkable individual. He has magnetism, plus. His zeal, enthusiasm, animation, hope and faith run over and inundate everything.

No man can argue with him. No man can dispute with him. Everyone has to agree with him—and everyone does. He is what he is. He was born to this work, and for this work, and considers himself divinely appointed. . . .

America has never produced a religious leader with the zeal and health and insight and patience and intellectual reach of this man. . . .

He is in touch with big people, and meets all classes and kinds of people on an equality. . . .

No man of recent times has shown such a magnificent affirmative spirit as this man Abdul Baha. . . .

He listens with much appreciation and sympathy and when he speaks it is slowly, distinctly, and most impressively. He knows what he is saying. His heart is full and his emotions are brimming, although kept well under control.

. . . this man's poise, power, unselfishness and world-wide vision mark him as something more than a religious enthusiast. . . .

He speaks many languages and certainly speaks English better than most Americans do. . . .

So he comes, seemingly out of college, fresh, uncontaminated by the world of work and worry.

He is reverential, respectful, filled with a great and holy zeal. And this zeal takes the form of a message of unification to the world.

There is no doubt, among thinking people, that this man represents, in a great degree, the growing and evolving spirit of our times. . . .

. . . the divine fire of this man's spirituality is bound to illuminate the dark corners of our imaginations and open up to us a spiritual realm which we would do well to go in and possess.[1]

On Monday morning, July 1, after prayer, He said to the Persian friends, "'This help and assistance are from Him [Bahá'u'lláh] and these confirmations are through His Bounty and Favor; otherwise we are nothing but weak servants. We are like flutes and all these tunes are from Him.'"

Later He said to a group of friends departing for the Green Acre Institute in Maine:

When you go to Green Acre you must have infinite love for each other, each preferring the other before himself. The people must be so attracted to you that they will exclaim, "What happiness exists among you!" and will see in your faces the lights of the kingdom; then in wonderment they will turn to you and seek the cause of your happiness. You must give the message through action and deed, not alone by word. . . . The cause of Baha' Ullah has not yet appeared in this country. I desire that you be ready to sacrifice everything for each other, even life itself; then I will know that the cause of Baha' Ullah has been established. . . .[2]

On Tuesday morning, as 'Abdu'l-Bahá walked in the park by the river near His house, a group of persons of Greek ancestry who were strolling nearby introduced themselves and began asking questions. 'Abdu'l-Bahá talked to them of the Greek philosophers and the meaning of the history of Greece. "Then," Maḥmúd recorded, "He exhorted and encouraged them to acquire the virtues of the world of humanity. The attraction of His Beauty was so great that they spontaneously bowed to its influence. They came to the assembly of Bahá'ís that night and joined the group of lovers."

The New York Times for that day and Wednesday noted, "Cuban Revolt Seems Over"; "Houdini's New Trick, Escapes from Huge Can of Water after Being Locked in Chest"; and "Woodrow Wilson Is Nominated for President."

And then came July 4. The mayor of New York asked 'Abdu'l-Bahá to be with him on the parade reviewing stand. 'Abdu'l-Bahá did not go, but sent the other Persian friends to represent Him.

After an evening meal in 'Abdu'l-Bahá's house honoring the birthday of Juliet Thompson's mother, the Master spoke of tests: "Even the sword is no test to the Persian believers. They are given a chance to recant; they cry out instead: 'Yá Bahá'u'l-Abhá!' Then the sword is raised. They cry out all the more, 'Yá Bahá'u'l-Abhá!' But some of the people here are tested if I don't say, 'How do you do?'"[3]

On Sunday, July 7, the New York Times carried an article headed, "Billion Dollar Subways World's Biggest Undertaking."

When one of the inquirers of Greek background asked 'Abdu'l-Bahá to accompany Him to a park outside the city where his friends were waiting to ask questions, 'Abdu'l-Bahá went with him. In the subway He said,

"'Man's nature must attain an inclination to ascend and not to descend.'"

Early that week 'Abdu'l-Bahá went to the Museum of Natural History and saw the enormous model of a whale. He commented, as Juliet Thompson recalled on July 12, "*He* could hold seventy Jonahs!"

During the sweltering July days 'Abdu'l-Bahá continued to receive the friends from morning until night, working with the Bahá'ís to deepen them, and to raise them up into a divine army that might spiritually conquer the world. He often prepared meals for them, prayed with them, walked with them in the garden near His house, notified the Eastern friends of the victories, introduced newcomers to the Faith, spoke before large audiences —giving of Himself in ways that would drain away ordinary physical energy, and, with the giving, demonstrating the example of never-ending sacrifice. He urged the unity of the friends and deepened them in the history and the Teachings of the Faith, using many hours for explanations and illustrations. At all times He reflected, like a many-faceted divine diamond, the various attributes which were part of the single light of God, descending on Him through the Blessed Perfection, Bahá'u'lláh.

He had asked Lua Getsinger to go to California to proclaim the Covenant; but she, eager to be with Him, delayed going and finally walked in poison ivy during the Unity Feast to prevent her departure. 'Abdu'l-Bahá sent her some fruit, and she was quickly cured. Again He directed her to go, and finally she did.

Mrs. Getsinger was not the only one to receive 'Abdu'l-Bahá's personal guidance and deepening. Every friend who came had precious moments with Him, for

His words and deeds were matched exactly to each one's needs. Juliet Thompson, who wished very much to have prayer beads used by Him, brought Him hers to use for a time. Later she found Him sitting with a lapful of beads brought by the friends. Hers He had given to someone else. Thus she learned another lesson.

'Abdu'l-Bahá searched every face and every heart, encouraging the beginners, urging the learners, directing the more advanced, opening vistas of the spiritual world to their inner vision, inviting them, by His words and examples, to enter this world, and, while walking on the earth, to react to the divine realities instead of the material facade that covered the true spiritual environment.

While He had already proclaimed the Faith in Chicago, Boston, Philadelphia, Cleveland, Pittsburgh, and other places, it was in New York that He stayed day after day, deepening those who came to Him, preparing them to develop new inner eyes, ears, hearts, and minds, bringing together interracial gatherings, trying to get the friends to see the spiritual qualities of each other as a reality. By Tuesday, July 16, Mahmúd observed, "His extended stay in New York had brought wonderful results among the friends."

Each individual's experience with Him was a thread weaving in and out of the experiences each of the others was having. It was this balance, this whole, that gave the completeness of 'Abdu'l-Bahá's example. He possessed an unparalleled ability for weaving together in a fabric of love and harmony the inner private development of the mass of individuals who surged to see Him, for making them part of the new World Order. He taught them so that the new community of believers would grow and develop and become self-perpetuating after His departure.

The friends from the West Coast who could not travel to the East to meet 'Abdu'l-Bahá sent telegrams beseeching Him to come. In July some of the Californians came in person asking Him to visit them.

On July 17, 'Abdu'l-Bahá chanted a prayer at the marriage of Harlan Ober and Grace Robarts, at which Howard Colby Ives officiated.

On July 18 *The Independent* magazine carried an editorial entitled "The Persian Prophet":

> The visit of Abdul Baha to this country is an interesting event even to those of us who do not see in Bahaism a new revelation destined to supercede the older faiths. It is interesting, at the least, to have brought visibly before us evidence that Asia, the aged mother of all the great religions of the world, has not yet become barren. For he who is now in our midst is by many millions of people today regarded as a prophet, "yea, and much more than a prophet." The number of his followers can, of course, be only vaguely estimated. . . . the foremost aim of Bahaism is unity. It would "the Two-and-Seventy jarring Sects" not "confute," but combine. . . .
>
> Bahaism is not to be classed with the freak or fake religions which arise among us or are brought to us from abroad. Perhaps there are among its American disciples some of the class who take up with Bahaism because bridge is going out. If so we may at least congratulate them on the change. Bahaism has proved its vitality, its reality, not only by inspiring its adherents to suffer martyrdom by the thousand for the new faith, but still more by inspiring them to live together in peace and harmony. . . .

As was stated in our issue of April 11, the Bab was executed at Tabriz in 1850; then arose one greater than he, Baha Ullah, who spent most of his life in prison, and his son and successor, Abdul Baha, now in this country, was only released from perpetual imprisonment by the Turkish revolution. He is an aged man now, with a long white beard and a saintly face, worn but peaceful. His bearing is simple and dignified, unembarrassed by unaccustomed surroundings, giving his message from a Christian pulpit to a strange audience in a foreign land with the same earnestness and naturalness as though he were addressing his disciples in Acre. To say "from a pulpit" is hardly correct, since he dislikes to occupy such an exalted position, preferring to put himself upon a level with his audience. Standing upon the floor or walking to and fro, he speaks quietly in Persian, which, sentence by sentence, is translated, tho at times his expressive features and gestures make the services of an interpreter superfluous. He wears a small white turban and a black robe over a white girdled garment. He greets the audience by touching his forehead repeatedly with the palm of the right hand and closes his sermon with a half-chanted prayer, standing and holding his hands upward and open, as though ready to receive the blessing he beseeches.

His message, coming from the most turbulent and dissentious country of the globe, is an appeal for love, peace and unity. He shows how strife and enmity defeat the aims of humanity in every field. "The aim of religion is fellowship and love, so taught His Holiness Christ, but said His Holiness Baha Ullah, if religion becomes the cause of enmity then surely is irreligion better than religion. Religious teachings are remedies, but when a remedy causes the disease it is worse than nothing." States are founded to secure a greater degree of co-operation among the people, but if states give rise to wars then are they altogether wrong. Language is designed to extend the scope of human intercourse, but this purpose is defeated when language is made a means of isolation and disagreement. There should be a common international language which all could learn and so the whole world be brought into communication. To say that there is a conflict between science and religion is false, for "how can the heart approve what the brain does not accept?" The diversity and discord that exists between the sexes is due to the false education and position of women in the past. "Women should be educated as men are and have the same rights in all things."

Such in essence is the Bahai doctrine, tho stripped of poetic imagery and illustration that grows in a Persian garden. A strange offshoot from Mohammedanism in these latter days—this religion of universal peace, mutual toleration and equal rights. Tho its lessons may be most needed in Islam, yet they are far from being superfluous to Christendom.[4]

'Abdu'l-Bahá continued to explain, in a multitude of ways so that all might understand, the object and goal of His endless work and teaching. On July 19, for example, He told the friends:

My weak constitution and excessive work are drawbacks. Otherwise it were possible that many extraordinary souls would have arisen among the friends. As long as such souls do not arise, the real object will not be accomplished. Devotion and capacity to work have been created to some extent in these friends. But the persons whom I mean have different qualities. . . . They [Mullá Ḥasan and Mullá 'Abdu'l-Laṭif] were deputized by the Mujtahids to see the Blessed Beauty at Mázindarán. The moment they approached Him they were so changed and their reality was so transformed and adjusted that they did not remain indifferent for a moment. After undergoing great troubles and persecutions Mullá 'Abdu'l-Laṭif was martyred at the altar of sacrifice. Similarly a blind Indian Sheik became so altered after his meeting the Beloved One that he was always found to be inebriated with joy and happiness. Such persons are required to rise for the Cause of God. Such persons are worthy of the field of service and devotion.

The next day He spoke extensively about the martyrs. On the following evening He was invited to the home of the Consul General of Turkey where He spoke to a group of Armenians.

When the July 20 issue of *Harper's Weekly* appeared on the newsstands, it included an article entitled, "A Ray from the East," by Charles Johnston:

During the past few months there has appeared at peace conferences, in fashionable pulpits, and at select meetings of devotees, a venerable Oriental with benign eyes and a patriarchal beard who is heralded as the head of a new world-religion. . . .

Before a word of comment on this teaching of Baha Ullah, let me illustrate also the style and method of the son and successor of the "Glory of God" by quoting a few sentences from one of his addresses, delivered in Persian at All Souls' Church in Chicago, in the beginning of May:

"Inasmuch," says Abdul Baha Abbas, "as the reality of religions is one, and the difference is one of imitations, but religion essentially is one, the existing religions must give up the imitations in order that the Reality may enlighten them all, may unite humanity. When people hold fast to that Reality, that Reality being one, all shall be united and agreed; all the religions then shall summon people to the oneness of the world of humanity; all the divine religions will proclaim equality of rights; all the divine religions will summon people to the mercy of God; all the divine religions will admonish people to virtue. The foundation is one, there is no difference therein. If the essentials of religion, therefore, be observed, peace shall be the result, and when we study conditions we find that the conditions existing are due only to imitations which have crept into religions, and the differences in the imitations have caused these various denominations and sects.

"And now let us consider the various people of the world. They all belong to one kind. . . . God has created all humanity; He has provided for all; He preserves all, and all are submerged in the ocean of His mercy. Inasmuch as we have a kind God, why should we be at war with one another?"

It must have become quite clear long ago to readers that we have here exactly the same thoughts, expressed in almost exactly the same words, as have made the material of religious urging and teaching for hundreds of years. Paul said, at Athens, before the sixtieth year of our era, exactly what Abbas Effendi repeats, in Chicago, at the beginning of the twentieth century.

Does it follow, then, because these two Persian teachers are repeating, in slightly varied phrase, the world-old and age-worn truths that their mission is the less real and valuable? By no means. The very fact that these men of strange race and alien tongue come to us and tell us, out of the depth of their hearts, what we have heard from the beginning, does much to bring the sense of unity that is the very center of their thought. It is a great and compelling thing to find a deeply religious man not of one's own faith and civilization. Such a one cannot fail to deepen our sense of religion. And these men have this in addition, that, holding the universal truths, they have honestly and in the face of dire perse-cution striven to carry them out. They live their religion, as well as teach it. This is their power.[5]

As He was preparing to depart for Boston and New Hampshire on July 22, the brother of the Khedive of Egypt, Prince Muḥammad-'Álí Páshá, arrived in the city. 'Abdu'l-Bahá visited him twice, and he returned the visits. The Prince later published in Egypt an account of his travels which referred to his meeting with 'Abdu'l-Bahá. He described 'Abdu'l-Bahá's "vast sagacity and infinite intelligence" and "His vast experience and wide knowl-edge" and concluded by saying, "He made me happy by His delightful talks."

11

New Hampshire

'Abdu'l-Bahá left New York at 8:00 A.M. on Tuesday, July 23, and arrived in Boston for a second visit at 3:30 P.M. He sent most of His entourage on to Dublin, New Hampshire, but He and a translator and secretary took rooms at the Victoria Hotel in Boston, where a public meeting was held at 6:00 P.M. After that He went to Mrs. Francis W. Breed's home and talked to a large group of people before returning to the hotel.

On Wednesday, July 24, He spoke with the visitors at His hotel room from 8:00 A.M. until noon, when He went to speak at the Golden Ring Club. A number of people crowded into the car afterward and asked Him questions during an hour-and-a-half drive. Another group was waiting when He returned to the hotel. Later that night He spoke to the Boston Theosophical Society.

The next day 'Abdu'l-Bahá spoke with more visitors until the late afternoon when He departed for Dublin, where He arrived at 7:00 P.M. and took up residence at one of Mrs. Arthur J. Parsons' two homes. Until August 16 He remained in Dublin, surrounded by green hills, flowering gardens, and flowing streams.

His days were spent in talking in detail with the persons who came from nearby and from distances, in speaking to local gatherings, and in writing the endless Tablets (letters) to people around the world. Again, He was taking time to deepen the friends, to inspire them, to raise them up, to teach them the spiritual meaning of life, to prepare them for the tasks that lay ahead, and to show them how to develop true happiness. He told the friends, on July 30, "'What captives of superstitions people are! What troubles and inconveniences they endure for the sake of name and fame! . . . They are sowing seeds in a barren land. Man ought to sow pure seeds in a fertile soil.'"

That same afternoon He said, "'We have not come to America on a pleasure trip but we are here to offer devotion to the Court of the Blessed Beauty. Wherever we are assisted in this devotion, we feel happy. A merchant is happy whenever his commodities find a market, wherever it may be.'"

Late that afternoon, 'Abdu'l-Bahá unexpectedly joined Mr. and Mrs. Joseph H. Hannen and Miss Alma Knobloch at Harrisville, three miles from Dublin. Mr. Hannen recorded the conversation:

> Abdul-Baha: "In returning [to Haifa], I will certainly go to Europe."
> Miss [Alma] Knobloch: "To Stuttgart?"
> Abdul-Baha: "Perhaps." (Laughing.)
> Mrs. Hannen: "They are supplicating for it."
> Abdul-Baha: "See how much we have moved from one place to another. How far New York is from here: Washington, Chicago, Philadelphia, the many places we have visited. And now these ladies have come to invite me to come to California. . . . A letter came yesterday from the Spiritual Assembly asking how it came that we went to other places and not there. Now

Mrs. [Emogene] Hoagg is going to build an aeroplane
and take me there. What do you advise? Shall I ride in
it?"

Mrs. Hannen: "It would not be very safe."

Abdul-Baha: "When I ride on it, it is the Ark of
Noah. This aeroplane will become the Ark of Noah."
(This was accompanied by an exchange of smiles which
showed Abdu'l-Baha's keen sense of humor.)[1]

On July 31, at 9:30 A.M., as 'Abdu'l-Bahá walked to and
fro on the veranda of His house talking to George Latimer,
Mr. Hannen recorded His words:

The Bahai must first be informed of the principles and
Teachings of Baha'o'llah, then go forth and spread the
Message. It is like unto a soldier, who must arm himself
with the buckler and armor, and then he enters the
battlefield to fight against the foe. But if he goes to fight
without arming himself, he will be defeated. The
Bahais are the Army of God. Their defensive armors or
weapons are: First, Faith; second, Assurance; third,
Severance; fourth, Complete Attraction to the Kingdom of Abha. If they are armed with these weapons,
they will gain the victory in whatever field they may
enter. As long as he is not equipped with these
weapons, he will not be successful. He must cut himself
entirely from all imitations. . . .

Mirza Ghorban Ali, who was one of the Seven
Martyrs, a man of great piety and learning, was a strong
Babi, but he was very fearful and timid. . . . the
enemies found him out somehow, and brought him into
the prison house. . . . the Prime Minister looked at him
and said: ". . . Are you ready to repudiate Ali Moham-

med (The Bab)?" Mirza Ghorban Ali, looking around, saw the executioner about fifteen feet from him, standing, and then he turned to the Minister and asked: "Whom shall I repudiate, Ali or Mohammed?" The Prime Minister became so angry that he ordered the executioners to take him away and kill him, and he left the presence of the Prime Minister with a serene face and a heavenly smile on his countenance. At such a time, a firm believer is known!"[2]

During His stay in New Hampshire 'Abdu'l-Bahá went to visit Mr. Henderson's summer school, five miles outside Dublin. When His car drove up, the students —ranging in age from twelve through eighteen and wearing knicker uniforms—came running out and surrounded the car. After speaking to them in the auditorium and inspecting their tents, He allowed them to photograph Him. After taking tea, the boys put on a gymnastic display, and 'Abdu'l-Bahá spoke at length on education.

While still in the Holy Land, 'Abdu'l-Bahá, in the presence of Miss Louisa Mathew of England and Mr. Louis G. Gregory, had noted that interracial marriage was a good way to overcome racial differences. On August 3, at a large meeting held near the Dublin River, He spoke of their forthcoming marriage. Mahmúd recorded:

When He mentioned the matrimony of Miss Mathew, a white woman, with Mr. Gregory, a colored man, which was going to take place . . . in the course of a few days, the white persons were astonished to see the influence of the Cause and the colored ones were pleased. Incidents like this were little less than miracles; in fact the splitting of the moon into two pieces seemed an easier accomplishment in the eyes of the Americans.

On the afternoon of August 5 among the people that crowded to be with Him in Dublin were two ladies who were hard of hearing. They asked the translator if they could sit near 'Abdu'l-Bahá in order to hear Him with their ear trumpets. 'Abdu'l-Bahá replied, "'Yes, the nearer they come, the better they will hear the Words of God. . . . It matters little in what way or by what means they hear it.'"

On August 6 a visitor told Him that her friends had warned her not to come lest she fall into a trap. 'Abdu'l-Bahá replied, "'God be thanked that we have been in this trap for sixty years and we are happy in it. . . . It is a trap that frees the people from the shackles of prejudice and superstitions. . . . it makes them the captives of the love of God and service to the Cause of the oneness of humanity.'"

After a meeting that same day when 'Abdu'l-Bahá had referred to the cow as the greatest of materialistic philosophers since she knows nothing beyond the sensory level of the animal, He and several others went for an automobile ride. Coming across a herd of cows the ladies said, "'Master, see how this crowd of philosophers is afraid of the car and is running before it,'" and 'Abdu'l-Bahá laughed. Maḥmúd noted, "As Americans like such jests, it became an oft repeated remark."

When a young man asked Him, on August 9, in what school He had learned His philosophy, 'Abdu'l-Bahá replied, "'In the school in which Christ learned it.'"

At the close of a meeting on August 10, after He had shaken hands with the crowd of people, He went with the Persians to another room and said, "'Come here, be seated.

Mrs. Parsons has sent tea, sweets and some fruits for you. Eat and drink.'" With a twinkle in His eyes, He continued:

> Oh! you are very badly off here! May God hear your complaint! Oh! you are in great trouble. To live in this manner, to dwell in such a house, to walk in such air, and to stay with such . . . respected friends is, of course, very hard for you. . . . See what I meant by the jest. What a wonderful table the Blessed Perfection has spread for His friends! Had kings come here they would have been served. But this favor and zeal of the friends would not have appeared for any one of them. These great men love you with heart and soul and serve you without any fear, hope, or expectation of reward. The poet has truly said that these things, namely, the demon, . . . the phoenix, . . . and the faithful friend are scarce. Yes, like the demon and the phoenix, the true friend is scarce. But under the shadow of the Word of God, the Blessed Beauty has produced such friends for you.

On Sunday, August 11, while eating at the home of one of the friends, after He had spoken in the Dublin Unitarian Church, 'Abdu'l-Bahá gave answers that were so well worded and so complete that some of the newcomers thought He had written them out beforehand and memorized them. On August 14 He told one audience, "'I desire the meeting more than you. Some of the disciples of Christ went to Roumania once and said, "We had a desire to see you so we have come from Jerusalem to this place." Now behold what a desire I had to see you; I traveled from East to the West.'"

On 'Abdu'l-Bahá's last full day in Dublin, His 127th day in America, He said to the crowd, in reviewing all the meetings He had held there, "'I have explained every question for you, delivered to you the message of God, opened the mysteries of the Books of God before you, established the immortality of the spirit and the non-perishability of the single elements, and explained for you the economic questions and divine teachings.'"

When they asked Him to stay longer, He replied, "'. . . I must go to Green Acre and other places. I must raise the voice of the Kingdom in all places. As the days of My life are limited in this world, I must go to many places and raise My voice to deliver the glad tidings of the Kingdom of Abhá.'"

The next day, Friday, August 16, 'Abdu'l-Bahá left Dublin at 10:00 A.M., had lunch at Nashua, New Hampshire, and reached Green Acre, in Eliot, Maine, in the afternoon.

12

Green Acre

'Abdu'l-Bahá stayed at Green Acre for one week. The school had been founded by Sarah Farmer and her father as a center for educational exchange; to it came spiritualists, philosophers, artists, and educators. When 'Abdu'l-Bahá arrived, the way to the main building was decked with multicolored lanterns. Five hundred people were waiting.

Again, day and night, He was occupied in virtually endless discussions with individuals who sought His presence and in speaking with larger groups on topics as diverse as the interests of the people present. Maḥmúd noted, on August 17:

> many of the fortune-tellers, spiritualists and ascetics, came there [to Green Acre] every year to spread their superstitious views. The address of the Beauty of the Covenant ['Abdu'l-Bahá] demolished and destroyed their cobwebs of superstitions. They were checked to such a degree that some of these imposters who in previous years delivered lectures contrary to the Cause of God, now came to His Holy Presence, bowed before Him and expressed repentence.

That evening 'Abdu'l-Bahá offered candy to some persons who refrained from eating certain kinds of foods. "'Food has nothing to do with faith,'" He told them. "'You should eat things which give you strength and enable you to acquire spirituality.'"

The next day, August 18, after 'Abdu'l-Bahá spoke, the chairman sat weeping; and, as He ended in prayer, one lady stood up and fainted. Leaving that meeting, 'Abdu'l-Bahá stopped to hear a group that was singing. He said to them, "'We listen always to your terrestrial music, now it would be well for you to give ear to our celestial songs.'"

On August 19 He was invited to a campsite by the river on the extensive grounds of Green Acre where a group of girls were pitching their tents. He sat on the grass and watched before addressing them.

The guests at Green Acre and the inhabitants of Eliot, Maine, were not the only people who sought out 'Abdu'l-Bahá. Some years before Fred Mortensen had escaped jail while awaiting trial and had been a fugitive for four years. He later wrote that he remembered being captured when he leaped over a thirty-five foot wall, breaking his leg, "to escape the bullets whizzing around about. . . ." He had been defended by Albert Hall, who had introduced him to the Bahá'í Faith. Fred recalled, "it was he who told me, hour after hour, about the great love of 'Abdu'l-Bahá for all his children. . . . Thus the Word of God gave me a new birth, made me a living soul, a revivified spirit."[1]

In August Mr. Mortensen had gone from Minneapolis to Cleveland for a printers' convention. He wanted to visit 'Abdu'l-Bahá at Green Acre, but he had no money.

Therefore, he jumped on a freight train and rode the rods via Buffalo and Boston. Fred later described his arrival at Green Acre:

> The Boston and Main Railway was the last link between 'Abdu'l-Bahá and the outside world . . . and when I crawled off from the top of one of its passenger trains at Portsmouth, New Hampshire, I was exceedingly happy. . . . My heart beating double time, I stepped onto the soil of that to-be-famous center, tired, dirty, and wondering, but happy. . . .
>
> Arriving at the hotel I found quite a number of people there, on the same mission, to see 'Abdu'l-Bahá. Being one of the last arrivals, I was looking around, to make myself comfortable, when someone exclaimed, "Here he comes, now." Ahmad Sohrab did the introducing and interpreting. When Ahmad introduced me to him, to my astonishment he looked at me and only said, "Ugh! Ugh!" not offering to shake hands with me. Coming as I had, and feeling as I did, I was very much embarrassed. After greeting several others and when about to go to his room, he suddenly turned to me and said in a gruff voice (at least I thought so), "Sit down," and pointed to a chair—which I didn't care to do, as elderly ladies were standing. But what was I to do! I meekly obeyed, feeling rebellious over what had happened. Such a welcome, after making that difficult trip! My mind sure was in a whirl.
>
> . . . It seemed but a minute until Ahmad came down and said, " 'Abdu'l-Bahá wishes to see Mr. Mortensen." Why, I nearly wilted. I wasn't ready. I hadn't expected to be called until the very last thing. . . . He welcomed

me with a smile and warm hand-clasp, telling me to be
seated, he sitting before me. His first words were,
"Welcome! Welcome! You are very welcome,"—then
"Are you happy?"—which was repeated three times. I
thought, why do you ask me that so many times? Of
course I am happy; didn't I tell you so the first time?

Then, "Where did you come from?"

Answer: "From Minneapolis."

Question: "Do you know Mr. Hall?"

Answer: "Yes, he told me about the Cause."

Question: "Did you have a pleasant journey?"

Of all the questions I wished to avoid this was the
one! I dropped my gaze to the floor—and again he put
the question. I lifted my eyes to his and his were as two
black, sparkling jewels, which seemed to look into my
very depths. I knew he knew and I must tell, and as I
answered I wondered what Ahmad thought—if I were
a little unbalanced.

I answered: "I did not come as people generally do,
who come to see you."

Question: "How did you come?"

Answer: "Riding under and on top of the railway
trains."

Question: "Explain how."

Now as I looked into the eyes of 'Abdu'l-Bahá I saw
they had changed and a wondrous light seemed to pour
out. It was the light of love and I felt relieved and very
much happier. I explained to him how I rode on the
trains, after which he kissed both my cheeks, gave me
much fruit, and kissed the dirty hat I wore, which had
become soiled on my trip to see him.

When he was ready to leave Green Acre I stood
nearby to say goodbye, and to my astonishment he

ordered me to get into the automobile with him. After a week with him at Malden, Massachusetts, I left for home with never-to-be forgotten memories of a wonderful event—the meeting of God's Covenant. . . .[2]

Concerning 'Abdu'l-Bahá's generosity to Mr. Mortensen, and other people as well, Maḥmúd wrote on August 20:

The Beloved One said [to Fred], "You are My guest." Every day He bestowed upon him kindness and . . . He gave him money for the expense of his journey. . . . He paid for many indefinable expenses which were never known to anyone. He summoned a speaker in New York and sent him twice to Chicago and the adjacent cities. On each occasion, although the person was rich, He gave him more than sufficient money to defray the expenses of his journey. In addition He contributed to the welfare of the poor and to the support of the churches [where He spoke] of every city in a liberal manner.

On August 19 'Abdu'l-Bahá "gave instructions for the nineteenth day feast for the following day and said, 'The entertainment for tomorrow is with Me.'"[3] On August 20, with Sarah Farmer, He drove around in an automobile to see places of historical interest, giving her flowers, and kissing her as He got out of the car. That afternoon He spoke to three hundred persons under "the Persian pines and cypresses" and then invited all to the Bahá'í home where they were His guests.

In a group of people who came to see Him on August 21 was a girl who said, "'I have come to beg your assistance.

Tell me what I am fitted to do so that I may occupy myself with it?'" He asked her, "'Do you believe in Me?'" When she replied, "'Yes,'" He answered, "'Be a perfect Bahá'í. Associate with Bahá'ís. Learn the teachings of Bahá'-u'lláh. Then you will be assisted in whatever you undertake to do.'" She responded, "'I am a good Jewess,'" and He told her, "'A good Jew becomes a Bahá'í. The foundation truth of the religion of His Holiness Moses and His Holiness Bahá'u'lláh is one. Turn yourself towards Bahá'u'lláh and you will get peace and tranquillity. . . .'" She threw herself at His feet and cried.

Another woman said, "'I am dejected today, I hate myself.'" 'Abdu'l-Bahá told her, "'It is a sign of progress. . . . If a man has a thousand good qualities, he must not look to them. He must search always for his shortcomings and attend to them. If a man has a strong building . . . but which has a small crevice in one of its walls, he will, no doubt, forget its adornment and firmness and will turn his whole attention to having that small defect removed.'"

On August 22, in another of the crowds of people who continually came, was a woman who had survived the *Titanic* disaster. She said, "'I am informed that you advised not to go by that boat.'" 'Abdu'l-Bahá replied, "'Yes.'" She asked, "'Did you know that it would happen thus?'" He responded, "'God sends a feeling of misgiving into man's heart.'"

On the day 'Abdu'l-Bahá left Green Acre, Friday, August 23, He said, "'We have finished our work here. We have sown the seeds. Many of the souls are attracted and will be changed.'" On the way out of town at 10:00 A.M., they stopped at Sarah Farmer's home to say good-bye. She fell weeping at His feet.

13

Montreal

'Abdu'l-Bahá arrived in Malden, Massachusetts, at 1:00 P.M. on August 23, and stayed for one week, making trips to Boston and Cambridge. As elsewhere, people in great numbers sought Him out, and He spoke to them individually and in groups. He was the kind, loving host, infusing in them by word and by action the seeds of what they could become.

Along with the numerous meetings in Miss Marie P. Wilson's home, where He stayed, and the other homes to which He was invited, He spoke to the New Thought Forum for the Metaphysical Club of Boston, lectured at the Franklin Square House on women's rights, addressed the Theosophical Society, and attended the wedding of Clarence Johnson and Ruby Breed.

The newspapers reported several events attended by 'Abdu'l-Bahá. The *Boston Evening Transcript*, on August 29, said:

> Interest out of the usual for a wedding was found in the address to the bridal couple and bestowal of his blessing by Abdul Baha Abbas, the Persian leader, who is touring this country propagating his new religion, based on

the brotherhood of man. He is a friend of the bride's
sister, Mrs. Ali Kuli Kahn, wife of the Persian chargé
de'affaires at Washington, and who formerly was Miss
Florence Breed. . . . Little Marzieh Khan . . . was
flower girl.

On August 31 the *Transcript* noted:

Abdul Baha Abbas . . . was the guest of honor at a
reception given on Thursday evening at her residence
in Malden by Mme. Beale Morey, the musician. There
were nearly a hundred guests present, for whom Mme.
Morey played at the piano an introductory musical
programme, following which Abdul Beha Abbas gave a
talk on the "Religions of the World," showing the points
of similarity of beliefs of different nations and their
relations in the forming of a universal brotherhood. The
hostess, Mme. Morey, in her travels in the Far East
studied into the various religions, including that of the
Hindoos, Buddhists, the fire worshippers and others.

'Abdu'l-Bahá left Malden and caught a train in Boston at
9:00 A.M. on Friday, August 30, for Montreal, Canada,
arriving there at midnight. He was met at the station by
William Sutherland Maxwell. Reporters and friends
packed the Maxwells' house waiting for Him, and Mrs.
Maxwell said that invitations and inquiries had been pouring in all day.

He remained in Montreal for ten days, living at the
Maxwells', and, then, despite their entreaties, moving into
the Hotel Windsor. The friends and inquirers flocked
around Him throughout His stay. He spoke at meeting

after meeting at the Maxwell home, and, among other places, at the Unitarian Church, at the St. James Methodist Church, and at the Socialist Club.

On Saturday, August 31, as He rode through town, 'Abdu'l-Bahá passed the cathedral. After going in to look at it, He told the friends, "'Behold what eleven disciples have done. How they effaced themselves! I exhort you to walk in their footsteps. When a person is severed, he is capable of revolutionizing the whole world.'"

That evening, after 'Abdu'l-Bahá had granted scores of interviews all day long, another group was waiting for private talks. Because He was so tired, the friends suggested that the remaining people should leave and return the next day. He answered, "'No, this is the time to work. We must not think of exhaustion or anything else. Let every one come to me.'"

On Sunday, September 1, as He prepared to leave for the Unitarian Church where He was to speak, 'Abdu'l-Bahá called one of the Persian friends to sit by Him in the carriage. The friend replied that there was plenty of room on another seat; but 'Abdu'l-Bahá insisted, "'Come and sit here. When I see some one selfish and hankering after rank, I observe these formalities for his correction merely. Everyone may sit wherever he wishes. These things are entirely unimportant.'"

At the breakfast on September 2 to which He invited a number of guests 'Abdu'l-Bahá said:

Come, we are in Montreal, Canada, in this home eating Persian pilau, which has been cooked by Mírzá Aḥmad and which has a taste and tale of its own. To be grateful for the blessings of God in time of want and trouble is important. In the abundance of blessings every one can be grateful. It is said that Sulṭán Maḥmúd cut a watermelon and gave a portion of it to Iyás. Iyás ate it cheerfully and expressed gratitude. When the Sulṭán ate a little of the same watermelon, he found it bitter. He asked Iyás, "How did you eat such a bitter watermelon and show no sign of dislike?" He answered, "I had eaten many sweet and palatable things from the hands of the Sulṭán and I thought it very unworthy of me to express dislike on eating a little bitter thing today."

He concluded:

> Man, who is immersed in the blessings of God, should not be grieved if he sees a little trouble. He should not forget the manifold divine bounties that are always pouring on him.

That same day 'Abdu'l-Bahá moved to the Hotel Windsor. When He prepared to return to the Maxwells' home for a meeting, the friends asked if they could call a carriage for Him. 'Abdu'l-Bahá took the streetcar, saying, "'Oh, it matters little. It saves expenses. There is a difference of one dollar in the fare.'" When He arrived at the Maxwells', He gave one pound to each of the servants.

As the translations of the newspaper articles concerning His address at the Socialist Club were read to Him on September 4, 'Abdu'l-Bahá said, "'This is all through the confirmations of the Blessed Beauty. Otherwise even if the King of Persia had come here he would not have been able to attract such meetings.'"

Maḥmúd recalled:

In the afternoon He came down . . . for a ride in the automobile. We were in attendance also. The automobile stopped at the foot of a mountain beyond the city limits. An elevator took us up. The mountainside was perpendicular like a wall. The Beloved said, "This hoist is like a balloon which flies in the air."

One felt nervous to look below. When we reached the top, the Beloved walked to and fro. It was a magnificent sight. The whole of the city lay stretched before us. . . . It seemed as if a beautifully painted picture were spread before the view.

Here the translation of additional accounts of the meetings published in the evening newspapers was read before Him. Suddenly He cried out, "Bahá'u'lláh! May I be a sacrifice at Thy feet. O Bahá'u'lláh! May I be offered up in Thy way! What a wonderful Cause you have founded! It satisfies every sect! Every sect testifies to Thy greatness. In the churches it excites a new commotion in the souls. It imparts spirituality to the spiritualists; makes Unitarians informed of the Reality of Unity; makes the socialists contented and grateful and inspires joy and happiness in the breasts of the peace-lovers. There is no sect or denomination which has any cause for sighing! One and all bow spontaneously before Your majesty. It is a miracle. It is the greatest force of the world of existence. It is the assistance of the Blessed Beauty. This is the greatest miracle."

'Abdu'l-Bahá also commented, in discussing the warm reception of His address, "'The greatness of the Teachings of Bahá'u'lláh will be known when they are practiced.

Not one out of a hundred has as yet come into force. The entire trend of your thoughts should be turned towards bringing these blessed Teachings into practice.'"

On September 5 the Bishop in Montreal visited 'Abdu'l-Bahá to express his pleasure at the meetings being held and his gratitude for "the address concerning the purpose of the Manifestation of Christ and the other holy Manifestations." 'Abdu'l-Bahá said, "'Tonight I shall speak in the Methodist Church. You may come if you wish.'" On the evening of September 6 Mrs. Maxwell reminisced with 'Abdu'l-Bahá: "'At the time when I was visiting 'Akká I despaired of the blessing of ever possessing children. Praise be to God! My desire and your prayer at the Holy Tomb of Bahá'u'lláh were accepted and I was blessed with a dear baby [Amatu'l-Bahá Rúḥíyyih Khánum].'"

The *Toronto Star Weekly* wrote of Him on September 7, in an article headed "ABDUL BAHA'S WORD TO CANADA":

What is it that strikes one most in this remarkable man? Is it his message . . . ? Is it his power of thought, his manner of expression, the privations he has endured? No; it is none of these. It is his great sincerity. He is a man with a mission, and he believes in it with all his soul. . . .

There was wonderful breadth and depth of feeling in that sermon [at the Unitarian church in Montreal]. It was not the message of a fanatic or a hermit, or a man unconversant with modern thought and modern life. It was Eastern, yet it was Western. . . .

He granted me an interview the following day. . . .

I then inquired if he intended to visit Toronto or any of the Canadian cities in the West, but he was afraid such would be impossible at this time. "But you may tell your people," he said, "that I am very pleased with your country. It is a prosperous and delightful land. . . . Surely, then, you should thank the good God for all his mercies to you."

He then took my hand in both of his and blessed me as a father would bless a son, with the same sincerity, the same depth of feeling, the same lofty purpose. For if this Persian dreamer, preacher, prophet, is anything, he is sincere, and his sincerity springs from a great sense of love and fellowship for man. He is a humanist of a high type; his church is the world.

"I cannot succeed," were his parting words, "without your help and the help of everyone who believes in the cause of universal peace and good fellowship among men; and, that you may not forget me and my cause in the days to come, I will ask you to accept a little gift from me."

So saying, he handed me a small parcel, which, later, I discovered contained a handsome gold ring. It fitted perfectly. . . .

'Abdu'l-Bahá had taught and exhorted and given of Himself during ten days of ceaseless activity in Montreal. On September 8, His last full day with the friends, He said, "'I have sown the seed. Now water it. You must educate the souls in divine morals, make them spiritual, and lead them to the oneness of humanity and to universal peace.'"

14

Buffalo, Chicago, Kenosha

After a dusty, hot, stifling ride, the train from Montreal to Buffalo stopped at Toronto, where 'Abdu'l-Bahá walked for a time on the platform. He arrived in Buffalo late at night on Monday, September 9; but, as He had instructed, the friends had not been informed. By the next morning, however, the reporters and friends were lined up outside the door of His hotel room. After hours of interviews He took a streetcar to Niagara Falls, at the request of the friends. There He ate some pears and grapes and walked in the park.

When His Persian companions suggested they stay in Buffalo for a period of time, He said, "'Even half a day is not possible. We have no time for amusements. We must keep ourselves employed with our work.'" Conversing on a variety of subjects, including cleanliness, He mentioned, "'I washed my hair with warm water without applying soap.'" Maḥmúd recorded, "We touched His musk diffusing locks which were in utmost cleanliness and luster."

After an evening meeting they all went out to view the city. Later He ate a little bread and cheese for supper before going to bed.

On Wednesday, September 11, after a series of interviews, 'Abdu'l-Bahá visited two of the friends who were
sick and distributed five dollars in coins to children who
gathered around Him on the street. That evening He
went to the Church of the Messiah. In the pastor's study,
before the meeting, the minister read an account of the
Faith he had written for the church paper. When he
concluded, 'Abdu'l-Bahá said, "'You have left nothing for
Me to say here tonight. You have written and published
everything in this booklet.'" After 'Abdu'l-Bahá spoke to
the congregation, the minister encouraged his parishion-
ers to go to Bahá'í meetings and to investigate for themselves.

An article appearing in the *Buffalo Express* on September
11 began, "ABDUL BAHA AN OPTIMIST: Thinks
Religious Unity And World Peace Will Come Within
Present Century." It continued:

> "Religious unity and world peace will come within
> the present century, by all means," said Abdul Baha in
> reply to a question by an Express reporter. . . .
> "Is that an inspired prophecy, or a plain human
> opinion?" ventured the reporter.
> "It is a divine prophecy," said one of Abdul's brown-
> robed and black-turbaned interpreters. . . . He spoke
> with solemnity and did not venture to repeat the ques-
> tion to his master. . . .
> "Are you a prince?" was another question asked of
> him in last night's interview.
> "I am a servant of God," was his answer.
> And that is what Abdul Baha means—the Servant of
> God. It is the title which he uses in front of his family

name which is Abbas—Abdul Baha Abbas, it reads on the hotel register.*

Whether or not one believes that the Abdul's predictions are the emanations of divine inspiration . . . one who listens to his addresses is bound to credit him with perfect sincerity and good faith in his mission of promoting religious unity and world peace.

The Abdul Baha came to Buffalo from Montreal late on Monday night. Although he had with him in New York and elsewhere in his tour of this country . . . a retinue of ten or a dozen native Persians, but three of them came with him to Buffalo. They registered as Dr. Ameen U. Fareed, Mirza (which means Mister) Ahmad Sorab and Mirza Mahmood Zarzhani. The former two are interpreters, the last a secretary. . . .

They returned to the hotel shortly after 8 o'clock. The hotel parlors were occupied by 50 or 60 persons . . . waiting to hear him speak at that hour.

The venerable missionary was too fatigued to attend just then, but in less than half an hour he came down from his rooms, attended by his secretary and interpreters. He seated himself at the speaker's table before the audience while one of his interpreters stood beside him. The other interpreter and the secretary seated themselves at each end of the table and with notebooks in hand began to take down his utterances in Persian shorthand, writing from right to left. . . .

The Abdul spoke in gutterals and nasals, and his interpreter made a running interpretation, stopping in the middle of long sentences when the Abdul stopped.

---

*Abbás was 'Abdu'l-Bahá's given name.

The translations were in perfect English and beautiful in their eloquence. . . .

So ending his discourse, Abdul Baha went to his audience and shook each member of it by the hand, blessing each in some Persian utterance. . . .

On Thursday 'Abdu'l-Bahá called the Persians together before dawn to pack, and they left for the train station. 'Abdu'l-Bahá left a tip with the manager for the bellboy who had served them previously. But to the taxidriver who wanted additional fare for driving Him to the station 'Abdu'l-Bahá paid no attention. He told the friends, "'A man may give $1,000 without minding it, but he should not yield even a dollar to the person who wishes to take it wrongfully, for such wrongful behavior is against justice. . . .'" His departing train sped past Niagara Falls and across the fields and valleys of the Midwest, until at 8:00 P.M. the lights of Chicago appeared. It was September 12.

The *Chicago Record-Herald* announced 'Abdu'l-Bahá's return, saying that He "will hold a series of meetings" and that "He is a guest at the home of Mrs. Corinne True of 5338 Kenmore avenue and is accompanied by a Persian secretary, an interpreter and two servants." A large group of demonstrative friends met Him at the train, and He drove to Mrs. True's home, where a crowd awaited Him.

The Independent magazine for September 12 contained a feature entitled, "America and World Peace," with the author listed as Abdul Baha Abbas. It opened with an editorial note and continued with 'Abdu'l-Bahá's responses to questions put to Him during an interview in New York on July 19:

[Abdul Baha Abbas, Persian prophet and teacher, courteously replied to the questions of a representative of THE INDEPENDENT by means of an interpreter. In spite of the lofty position ascribed to him by his followers, his interest in ordinary human affairs is keen. He was dressed in flowing robes and turban, which accorded well with his square cut grey beard. His blue eyes are frank, lively and humorous, his figure of medium height and slight, but erect and graceful in spite of his sixty-eight years. When he was in London he preached in the City Temple and in St. John's, Westminster, and in the United States he has been invited to the pulpits of various denominations. . . .—Editor]

I am very pleased with America and its people. I find religion, high ideals, broad sympathy with humanity, benevolence and kindness widespread here, and my hope is that America will lead in the movement for universal peace.

The people of this land enjoy many blessings. Day by day they are advancing and progressing, their fortunes are in their own hands, their patriotism is strong, they enjoy freedom in a superlative degree. They are not restrained by ignorance or the weight of old customs, nor are they tyrannized over by circumstances or fear of neighboring nations. In a hemisphere they are supreme, and as kindness is their natural disposition, the world will expect them to bear the banner of the peace movement.

Such leadership would be in accord with their own history and the principles on which their government is founded. . . .

I am here in this country making an appeal on behalf of universal peace, unity, love and brotherhood. I do not know how many Bahaists there are in America or in the world. There are no statistics in regard to this matter. If figures have been published they are without authority. . . .

Is peace always desirable? Undoubtedly it is. What is best in a family—peace or strife? Every good man will answer that family peace is best. So it is also with a nation, and so it is also with the whole world. In the United States of America forty-eight countries or States are gathered, living in peace with each other, and their enlightenment, happiness, progress and civilization serve as a model and inspiration to all men. It was not always so. Before Washington freed this country there were many wars and much strife and jealousy among the colonies. All that has gone, and peace, happiness and progress have come with union. The States support, love and are proud of one another, and what America has done, the rest of the world can do, following the example of America.

But would it be practicable for a country to lay down its arms and submit itself to the will of its neighbors —would not such a country be robbed and abused? Assuredly it is not practicable for a single country to disarm and trust the other nations to do justice for the sake of justice. Universal peace must be brought about by means of agreement among the great powers. They must assemble in convention, represented by their best and wisest men, and they must bind themselves by the strongest pledges and promises not to make war. Each should maintain an army and navy, but very small, merely enough to enforce order in its own territory. . . .[1]

On September 13, when some of the Persian friends remarked to 'Abdu'l-Bahá that "there was tea better" than that served by Mrs. True, 'Abdu'l-Bahá replied, "'This is the best tea of all, because it has been prepared with love.'" Talking about expenditures, He said, "'Sometimes I give away as much as $1,000, if I have it, but at another time I do not spend even a single dollar. This is a matter of managing the affairs.'"

Many people came to entreat Him to speak to various organizations, but He refused most of them because of lack of time. Referring to previous meetings, He told one gathering, "'Some took exception with me and asked why I sought to cultivate love between the whites and the colored. . . . When the people fondle an animal day and night, why do they not associate with a sensible man?'" On Saturday, September 14, among other things, He spoke of the Covenant and later addressed the Theosophical Society.

On Sunday 'Abdu'l-Bahá and His entourage prepared to leave for Kenosha, Wisconsin. They had to transfer trains en route, and somehow missed the second train. The friends were sorry, but 'Abdu'l-Bahá said, "'There is wisdom in it.'" They left by the next train, and on the way came upon the wreckage of the train they had missed; it had collided with another train. 'Abdu'l-Bahá said, "'The protection of the Blessed Beauty was with us,'" and then narrated the episode of leaving Alexandria for America, saying, "'Some of the people proposed that we leave via London by the S.S. *Titanic*, which was wrecked on the same voyage. The Blessed Beauty guided us to come direct.'"

In Kenosha 'Abdu'l-Bahá talked with the friends first and then addressed the Congregational Church. He departed Monday morning, September 16, to return to Chicago, where He moved from Mrs. True's home to a hotel. On the way there He said, "'I am bearing these hardships of traveling so that the Cause of God may push on uncontaminated. For I am still anxious about what is going to happen after Me.'"

On Tuesday morning 'Abdu'l-Bahá left Chicago for California. Traveling with Him were Dr. Amín Faríd, Mírzá 'Alí-Akbar, Mírzá Ahmad Sohrab, Mahmúd, and Fujita. Mahmúd noted: "Mírzá 'Alí Akbar Nakhjavání who was granted permission to accompany the Beloved in His travel to California arrived from Malden and joined Mr. Fujita of Japan and other attendants at 10:00 A.M. when the train left from Chicago. A number of the friends gathered around the Brilliant Face supplicating divine confirmations and aid to render service to the Cause of God."

15

Minnesota,
Nebraska,
Colorado, Utah

'Abdu'l-Bahá and His entourage traveled most of Tuesday, September 17, on the train toward Minnesota. "In these days," Maḥmúd noted, "the Holy Being appeared to be sad and depressed. At one time He said, '. . . The Ark of the Cause is invested with tempests and storms from all sides. But the confirmations of the Pre-existent Beauty are with us.'"

At 9:00 P.M. Mr. Albert Hall and some others got on the train several stops away from Minneapolis and rode with them. 'Abdu'l-Bahá told the reporters waiting for Him when they arrived that He would see them the following morning and went to the Hotel Plaza. When the friends told Him of many speaking invitations, He replied, "'Oh no, we cannot stay more than two days. We come to your city to put a fresh spiritual unction into it. We come to sow the seeds, to make the people awake, to deliver to them the greatest news and then to depart from the city. In this short space of time our work is to proclaim the Cause of God, and, Praise be to God, its results are becoming evident, and powerful confirmations are descending upon us day by day.'"

The next day, Wednesday, September 18, 'Abdu'l-Bahá spoke in the assembly hall of the hotel, at the

Commercial Club, and later at a synagogue. The following morning He also visited the Walker Art Gallery. One of the things they viewed were ancient tear vials from Phoenicia. 'Abdu'l-Bahá observed:

> Behold! These bottles have outlasted the bodies of men under the earth. When riches are increased, the westerners begin to collect antique things to render service to the world of art. But when the Persians get a little money they keep one hundred horses in their stables, give themselves up to pomp and show and engage themselves in satiating their selfish desires and avarice. From the point of view of serving the Cause, both attitudes are useless. . . . Ten persons instructed in the Cause of God would become the cause of eternal honor and happiness as well as the source of everlasting life.

He was then driven to St. Paul by Dr. Clement Woolson at whose home He spoke with the friends. He returned to Minneapolis for another meeting that night.

All of the major newspapers of Minneapolis carried articles about His activities. Concerning His traveling, the September 18 *Minneapolis Tribune* indicated that "Albert H. Hall received a telegram from Abdul Baha last night [September 17, the night He arrived] announcing his coming." On September 19 the *Minneapolis Journal* reported:

> Long before the other guests at the Plaza hotel were astir today, Abdul Baha Abbas, head of the Bahaists of the world, who believes and teaches the eventual harmony and unity of religious mankind, . . . was up

and about in parlor 603, pacing quietly across the room and back, and pausing occasionally to look meditatively out across Hennepin avenue into Loring Park. At 7 a.m. the five members of his party called at his parlor to pay their respects. Dr. Clement Woolson of St. Paul called on behalf of the St. Paul Bahaists and Dr. H. S. Harper and Albert H. Hall of Minneapolis came next. Mrs. R. M. Passmore and Mrs. H. G. Harrison, who had been in the country where Baha's influence is greatest in their foreign travels, and who had known well in advance of his coming, sent him messages of welcome to Minneapolis. Dr. S. N. Deinard of Jewish Reform temple called to pay his respects and see if it would be possible to arrange for the Bahaist leader to address the Jewish people of Minneapolis. . . .

. . . He smiled faintly, and two beautiful, large hazel eyes looked about the room. He rose from the divan on which he had been sitting and walked towards the window. Except that his complexion is dark and he is short of stature, he looked not unlike the portraits of General Robert E. Lee, the contour nose being particularly striking. . . .

. . . he shook hands with several visitors, and his hand felt like a silken glove. H. S. Fugeta, a Japanese from Cleveland, who had joined the party at Chicago, came in and knelt beside a window chair, where Abdul Baha had seated himself, and the leader placed his hands on the head of the kneeling man and uttered prayer in Persian. The syllables were strangely effective and rhythmetrical. Mirza Ahmed Sorab translated it aloud.

"Your spiritual growth is noteworthy; you are becoming stronger; your spirit is awake and you will be happy," was the less poetic English rendition of part of it.

On September 20 the *Tribune* reported, under the heading, "PROPHET OF GLORY VISITS MINNE-APOLIS":

Groups of curious people watched the progress through Loring park yesterday of an aged man with white turban and a flowing white beard, who walked with his hands behind his back, and was followed by a group of fez-crowned men, who spoke in a low voice and paid the aged man great deference.

Passersby who were attracted by the strange group followed through the park at some distance.

The aged man was Abdul Baha, from the Far East, "Prophet of Glory" and head of the new religion whose followers seek universal peace. Abdul Baha is stopping . . . with his four disciples. . . . Two of his disciples are from Persia, one from Russia and one from Japan.

Abdul Baha is one of the most picturesque religious figures in the Orient. He is 68 years old and was imprisoned for 50 years for his beliefs. The Baha has several hundred followers in the Twin Cities and thousands in the United States. Albert H. Hall of Minneapolis is one of the principal followers, and Mrs. H. McCutcheon and Dr. H. S. Harper of Minneapolis are also numbered in his following.

'Abdu'l-Bahá left Minneapolis on Friday, September 20, seeing Dr. Woolson again when the train stopped in St. Paul.

During the trip to Omaha 'Abdu'l-Bahá said:

A man fully learned, deeply attracted and wholly severed like some of the first Persian teachers is required for these American countries. The Cause of God must find a solid foundation. . . . Then the confirmations of the Kingdom of Abhá will envelop these nations and a resurrection will be set up. Up to the present time it has not reached the mark I desire. It rests wholly on the confirmations of the Kingdom of Abhá and on the sanctified souls among the friends. God is my witness! If a person draws only one breath in a state of complete severance, it will bear fruits whether it be after a thousand years.

It was late at night when 'Abdu'l-Bahá reached Omaha, and He went immediately to the hotel.

The next morning, September 21, as they were having tea in the room, they read the news of the first Balkan War. 'Abdu'l-Bahá observed, "'Our war is the best of all. We conquer all. At the time a crown of thorns was placed on the head of the Christ, He saw the crowns of kings under His feet. Now I see all the powers and nations vanquished and lost in the desert while the Cause of God is victorious over all. The divine Manifestations see with their eyes all the coming events of the world.'"

He spoke with reporters and wrote a number of Tablets before a lunch of soup at the hotel. Then He prepared to leave for Lincoln, Nebraska, to visit William Jennings Bryan, who had tried to see 'Abdu'l-Bahá when he traveled near 'Akká but had not been able to do so. When 'Abdu'l-Bahá and His entourage reached the train station, the train had already departed. As they waited for the next train, a man came running up, saying that he and the other friends in Omaha had received a telegram from the Bahá'ís in Minneapolis, informing them that 'Abdu'l-Bahá was in their city. The man ran to find his companions who were also searching for 'Abdu'l-Bahá; when they returned, they all talked together on the train platform.

In Lincoln 'Abdu'l-Bahá telephoned the Bryan home. Mrs. Bryan explained that her husband was not at home but that she and her daughter would like to receive Him. He rented a car, drove to the Bryan estate, and had tea with Mrs. Bryan, who asked Him to pray for the success of her husband's endeavors.

Returning to a hotel in Lincoln, He sat in the lobby. Many people who had read the articles in the newspaper came and introduced themselves and asked questions until His train departed at 11:00 P.M. On board, the friends tried to persuade Him to take pullman accommodations; but He said, "'We must all be in one place. The only purpose of this journey is to serve the Cause of God. We will all sleep on our seats.'" They spent the night in the chair car, riding toward Denver.

At 2:00 P.M. on Monday, September 23, as 'Abdu'l-Bahá arrived at the Denver station, He was greeted by Mr. and Mrs. Ashton and other friends and went to the Shirley Hotel. He asked reporters who came to His third floor room to return a short time later, which they did, at 5:00 P.M.

At 8:00 P.M. 'Abdu'l-Bahá went to the home of Mrs. Sidney Roberts and spoke with the friends. He also accepted an invitation to speak in a church and asked the others who wished interviews to visit the hotel the next morning.

After the morning sessions on September 24 He walked through the park. Many people stopped and looked, and some took photographs as He passed by. One of the friends remarked that, with their diversity of Eastern and Western clothes, people were looking upon the sight as a comedy. 'Abdu'l-Bahá laughed, "'Yea, it is heavenly fun, a performance of the Kingdom and a wonderful theater.'"

When He went by train to the suburban home of Mrs. Clark in the afternoon, again some observers were whispering about them. 'Abdu'l-Bahá told the friends to tell them, "'We are neither Turks nor Arabs; neither of the East nor of the West; but we are of heaven and of God.'"

One person in the crowd at the Clark home asked, "'What shall I do to become a true servant?'" 'Abdu'l-Bahá answered:

Act according to the teachings of His Holiness Bahá'u'lláh, and don't content yourself with the reading of them only. What I say is not even a mist from the ocean of the Supreme Pen and not even a drop from the depthless sea of the Bounty and Favor of the Beauty of Abhá. I have brought only the Teachings of Bahá'u'lláh to this country which will induce people to investigate reality, to render service to humanity, to endeavor to bring about international peace, to exert every effort to guide humanity, to show kindness to all creatures, and to raise the voice of the Kingdom. A human being must be characterized with divine attributes and must enter the concourse of the exalted ones. These Teachings are only a drop from the sea concealed in the Hidden Words. We must pray for each other. If we act according to the divine instructions, we shall shine like lamps. Woe be to the person, who is aware of the Teachings of Bahá'u'lláh and knows them to be the cause of eternal salvation and divine nearness but still he does not act according to them. It is incumbent upon us to endeavor day and night to follow the Teachings of God. This is the cause of eternal honor, divine favor, glory of mankind, and everlasting life.

To a question about His health, He responded, "'We have not traveled for rest and diversion. We have come to raise the voice of the Kingdom of Abhá. . . . If we rest for a few years what will come forth?'"

The *Denver Post*, on the preceding day, had run an article headed, "Negro Invasion Stirs Dwellers Along Kalamath—West Denver Neighborhood Proposes to Take Preventative Action." On September 25 there appeared an article in the *Post* entitled "ABDUL BA-HA ABBAS—PERSIAN TEACHER—TO CONVERT DENVER." The reporter, Frances Wayne, wrote:

A Man of God has come to town.

With the arrival yesterday of Abdul Ba-ha Abbas, a quicker spirit of tolerance, of brotherly love, of sincerer charity, of all those virtues which lift man above the beast was given wing and must, before his departure, have its effect upon every man and woman who comes within the radius of this wise man of the East.

Abdul Ba-ha entered the city without any of the glitter or pomp which is the attribute of nobility. He came . . . companioned by five devoted servants of the faith he preaches and by a reputation for sanity and holiness which makes of the most hardened cynic a respectful spectator.

It was with a sense of levity that I received the assignment to call on the Ba-ha.

"Another of those Oriental teachers and prophets

come to work on the emotions of women and long-haired men," I thought. "Another of those cunning gentlemen of Persia, who have deep wisdom concerning the spiritual strivings and material cupidities of this, our native land."

In such fettle I approached the presence of his apartments at the Shirley. In a far corner of the room, leaning back in his chair as though oppressed by a great weariness, his white beard flowing over his breast, his brown hands, carrying one simple jeweled ring, folded, and his eyes sending a kindly greeting toward the door, sat the Ba-ha. . . .

There was nothing theatrical, nothing spectacular in the scene. The atmosphere was vital with that brand of religion which can emanate only from one who is utterly pure in heart; who has found the truth by mining his way through great tribulation and whose life has been purged of all dross by the length and unselfishness of it.

The story of this man is rich in romance. Imprisoned for twenty years, exiled after that because he proclaimed the doctrine of brotherly love, equality of all men and the need of a recognition of the value of a spiritual life, his estate confiscated, he set out to give the message to the world at large. . . .

. . . Dr. Ameen U. Fareed, the interpreter . . . brings a flowing radiance and beauty to the Ba-ha's sentiments expressed in Persian which can only be comprehended by hearing.

"Why was that man imprisoned?" I asked Dr. Fareed.

"Why was Christ crucified?" he answered quickly. "The truth always has to fight its way through blood and human suffering, and the truth that the Ba-ha has to deliver is no exception."

Abdul Ba-ha is, first of all, a constructionist. He believes that the time of building is at hand and to this end war among the nations must cease. Looking upon his audience of visitors this morning he said, speaking through his interpreter.

"This is the Lord's supper. Material food is of little importance. It is knowledge, comprehension, good deeds, knowledge of God, the virtues of the human world, the perfection of the kingdom—this kind of food is acceptable. Whenever you desire to give a reception for me prepare such a table. Such food of companionship gives enrichment to the spirit; makes men more heavenly and suffers the world of humanity to become illumined."

That America shines in the vision of the Ba-ha as a great hope, but that it must wake to its shortcomings if its destiny is to be great, was indicated in this statement:

"The country of America is a good country. From every standpoint material happiness has been prepared for the people. Vast and spacious is this continent and it is overflowing with the blessings of God. In this continent you find all blessings and freedom discovers its highest fruitage. It should be a continent of happiness and comfort, but it is in need, however, of influences of a divine civilization. It needs the sun of reality. It is in need of spiritual culture, education, in need of the virtues of the ideal, in need of the effulgences of the kingdom of God that its people may become reinforced to institute universal peace and become enabled to serve the world and humanity.

"America must wake up so this people may cause the

spiritual progress of the world, its lights may shine, hearts become illumined and virtue revealed."

The Ba-ha talks with a strong voice, sitting moveless as he speaks and waits for Dr. Fareed to pass on his message. . . .

Certainly Denver has not in the past been honored by the presence of a Godlier man than this simple hearted Persian, whose only weapon, whose only charm is the Word. This he gives unto his hearers in that ornate, courteous form that is like rich embroidery. Last night the Ba-ha held a reception at the home of Mrs. Sidney Roberts, in Sherman street. Tonight at the Divine Science church at West Thirty-eighth and Perry street he will give an address and tomorrow night arrangements have been made for a meeting at the Shirley hotel, to which the public is invited.

"If you have a word or an essence which a brother has not, offer it with the tongue of love and kindness. If it is accepted the end is attained. If not with regard to him, deal not harshly, but pray."

The above is one of those delicate sentiments offered by the Ba-ha in parting, and which it might be well for every man and woman in this city of many strifes to cut out and paste in their hats or on their mirrors.

For the evening meeting on September 24 at the Church of Divine Science the *Denver Post* placed a car at the disposal of 'Abdu'l-Bahá. On the way there, He told the friends that the invitation to the church and the use of the automobile were confirmations that should cause them to become more self-effacing and unconcerned with worldly things, for these confirmations were not due to them personally, but to God, and that ""These burning lights which you see will become dark at once if the bounty of their origin is severed from them.'"

After a meeting the next day, September 25, He took a walk, and then spoke with the crowds who had gathered. To one person He said, "'Man is like a bird which is in the cage. A bird cannot get freedom by merely knowing that there are pure breezes, spacious firmament, beautiful gardens, pleasant parks and fountains outside. It must get a power to break the cage and to fly into the pleasant firmament.'" That afternoon He spoke at the home of Mrs. Roberts and that night at a public meeting at the Hotel Shirley.

The next day, September 26, the train left Denver heading west. At 2:00 A.M. He got off at Glenwood Springs and took rooms at the Hotel Colorado.

After morning prayers and tea 'Abdu'l-Bahá and His companions strolled around the beautiful grounds, surrounded by towering mountains. Then they went to the bath houses and bathed in the hot springs water. 'Abdu'l-Bahá said, "'We have been in many places during this journey but we had no time to see the sights. We had not even a moment's rest. Today, however, we have had a little respite.'" As they came out and looked at the river and mountains, 'Abdu'l-Bahá said, "'May God have mercy on the tyrants who kept the Blessed Beauty in prison for forty years. Such scenes were loved by Him.'"

He indicated that it would be well to have lunch in the central garden of the U-shaped hotel. The manager came just then and, without being asked, ordered the waiters to set up tables and serve lunch to them in the garden. As they ate, they could be seen from all areas. People began to speak to them and recognize them from the pictures and articles that had appeared in the Denver newspapers.

They started coming to Him by groups to talk with Him.
Later the *Star of the West* would report the consummation
on that day of the interracial marriage about which
'Abdu'l-Bahá had spoken in New Hampshire. At noon on
September 27 Louisa Mathew and Louis G. Gregory "were
happily married in New York City. . . . the bridegroom
said, 'Verily, we are content with the Will of God;' the
bride responded, 'Verily, we are satisfied with the Desire
of God.'"[1]

Among the telegrams that arrived in the late afternoon
was one indicating that Thornton Chase, the first American Bahá'í, was ill in a hospital in Los Angeles.

'Abdu'l-Bahá left Glenwood Springs on the train about
midnight and arrived in Salt Lake City the next afternoon,
September 28, where an agricultural convention was in
progress. Newspaper reporters, learning that He was unexpectedly in the city, sought Him out the following
morning and interviewed Him. Then He visited the agricultural exposition, looking at the equipment for plough-
ing and irrigation, asking about their uses and prices, and
surveying the displays of vegetables, grains, and fruits.
He bought some seeds to send to the Holy Land.

In Salt Lake City, too, the friends came in search of
'Abdu'l-Bahá. Feny E. Paulson has recorded her en-
counter:

> Travelling from Missoula, Montana, by the Chicago,
> Milwaukee, Ry., making a connection with Oregon
> Short Line going south, I arrived in Salt Lake City in a
> little less than twenty-four hours. The accommodations
> secured at the Young Women's Christian Association
> were exceedingly modest in furnishings. The room was
> so large that the four occupants were lost to each other.

The entrance hall was crowded with scaffolding, tar-pauline [sic], and canvas, light dim—all dirty because of the remodeling. Then the food: A dead fly in the German fries, a chicken wing with all the feathers (so it seemed), roaches at the soda fountain; I was grateful for the hard rolls and tea.

The telegram sent me announcing the date of arrival [of 'Abdu'l-Bahá] failed to state the name of the railroad: whether Grand Central and in which of the five sections, or the Oregon Short Line. Hence I spent most of my second day making the street car circuit, station to station, reading schedules of train arrivals.

'Abdu'l-Bahá arrived in the late afternoon . . . on one of the late sections of the Grand Central R.R. With Him were Mírzá Maḥmúd, His secretary, M. 'Alí-Akbar, M. Sohrab, Dr. Faríd and our Japanese Bahá'í friend, Fugita. 'Abdu'l-Bahá was wearing the customary 'abá and turban; the others fezes. It was an oriental picture in an occidental setting I saw at the far length of the station platform where the day coach passengers usually alight from trains. 'Abdu'l-Bahá liked to ride in the day coach and, too, it was less costly. They awaited my approach. The Master's powerful greeting: "Alláh-u-Abhá!". . . .*

It was decided to ride in the motor stage of the new Salt Lake City Hotel. On this ride the Master inquired of my trip down from Montana and then replied: "I will pray at the Threshold of the Blessed Perfection that you will always be taken care of." . . . The Salt Lake City

---

*Alláh-u-Abhá is an Arabic phrase meaning "God is All-Glorious." It is used as a greeting among Bahá'ís.

Hotel was very expensive and 'Abdu'l-Bahá was very economical.

Our group walked to the Kenyon Hotel where the price was more satisfactory. The room 'Abdu'l-Bahá used as reception room had a roll-top desk across the room near one end, and chairs on both sides against the two walls. No doubt it was used by salesmen to exhibit their goods.

It was the week of the convention of the Mormon Church; [and] the annual State Fair. The city was thronged with people from Utah, adjoining states, and beyond. According to M. Sohrab (whom I knew in Washington, D.C. as Persian translator of Tablets from the Master), the following day 'Abdu'l-Bahá stopped at the Mormon Tabernacle where the National Irrigation Congress was in session and where 'Abdu'l-Bahá was invited to a seat on the speakers' platform with those prominent in irrigation work. 'Abdu'l-Bahá soon left and attended the State Fair the remainder of the day. The program for this busy week called for a parade with beautiful electrically lighted floats in Agriculture motifs. . . . The parade used the street car tracks and so these were roped off. The sidewalks on both sides of the street, the windows and balconies of the business blocks were crowded with people eagerly waiting for the dark of the night to behold the spectacle. Attention was focused on that roped-off open space—when at dusk the flowing-robed figure of the Master with majestic bearing followed by His oriental companions, walked up the open space. A reporter responded to the unusual happening. The following day there appeared a first-page story in the paper. . . .

The following day I received the phone call I had been awaiting. The interview took place in the small room with the roll-top desk and chairs. Recall my mentioning the dirty hall at the Y.W.C.A. and the battle I had with food? The Master's first words were, "Luxury and comfort are not the all-important things in this life."

The Master served tea, saying, "This is the Lord's Supper you are having with Me." . . .

He also said, "I am your Father." That was to take the place of the father I had never remembered, and whom I had so often tried to recall.

'Abdu'l-Bahá was the Supreme Psychiatrist.

At the end of the interview the Master took a Bahá'í stone, pressed it to His forehead, then placed it on each of my eyes, His lips moving silently in a prayer or blessing. He also gave me a locket-sized likeness of Himself as a father gives a treasure to one of His children.

. . . Although the details of each person in the presence of 'Abdu'l-Bahá are individually different, they are the means to the same end—spiritual progress. Incidents forgotten and hidden in the recesses of one's being, in His presence, are in a flash perceived and unobtrusively aired, alchemized as it were, removing veils that inhibit necessary spiritual development. The problems and burdens that were but stepping stones in the past become non-essentials in the light of His divine love.

The interview was over. M. Sohrab asked me to accompany him while he shopped for food on their trip from Salt Lake City to San Francisco. I recall only that he ordered a leg of lamb to be roasted and called for. . . .

During the long wait in the passenger station 'Abdu'l-Bahá spoke in Persian until the train pulled in. Of the region in which I lived then, He said, "It is dark, very, very dark." He asked me, "You will write Ahmad?" Each of the four letters to Ahmad during World War I, after 'Abdu'l-Bahá's return to Haifa, brought a blessed Tablet from the Master.

He gave our Bahá'í friend Fugita instructions to remain to see that the baggage was safely on the train following and bade me stay with him. 'Abdu'l-Bahá left. Destination San Francisco. After a short stay, it irked me to remain longer even with Fugita's good company. Needless to say, any travel I have done since has brought me trouble and weeks and even months of delay with baggage. Life would be easier if we knew the wisdom of obedience. Lack of obedience is a great weakness. . . .[2]

On Monday morning, September 30, 1912, the *Salt Lake City Tribune* printed an article headed, "COMES TO LECTURE ON BAHAI RELIGION: Leader of Movement Will Explain Tenets to People of Salt Lake":

Abdul Baha Abbas, leader of the Bahai movement, which he says has 10,000,000 followers in the world, is in Salt Lake City. He is making a tour of the United States and plans to lecture on his religion here.

The principal tenets of the Bahai doctrines are the brotherhood of man and the fatherhood of God; the establishment of universal peace, the creation of a uni-

versal language and the establishment of a tribunal to
which all the nations in the world would come to settle
arguments. Its followers must seek out the truth in all
matters of religion and conduct for themselves. They
must have no pre-conceptions, handed down from their
fathers, but must search and decide the truth for themselves.

Abdul Baha is the son of the founder of the Bahai
movement, Baha-Ollah. He is a Persian. His native
government imprisoned him and his father in Acca,
Syria, where the son was held in exile for forty-two
years. Upon the dethronement of Abdul Hamid in
Turkey, the young Turks released Abdul Baha from his
Syrian prison and he was again allowed to go forth and
preach his doctrines.

He arrived in this country with his suite on April 11
of this year and has been making a lecture tour of the
country. Attired in his flowing native robes of a somber
gray, with a white fez on his broad brow, he presented a
striking appearance as he walked the downtown streets
last evening, followed respectfully by his attendants.

'Abdu'l-Bahá rode all day on Monday, September 30,
traveling to California. Among the many things He spoke
of to His companions, Maḥmúd recalled His saying,
"'The Cause of God is penetrating and ere long it will
surround the whole world. I see the expanse of America
full of Bahais. Formerly when we asserted in the East that
international peace was a necessity the people laughed at
us. Now behold the congresses of peace that have come
into existence. The law of God is the panacea for all
ills. . . .'"

At Green Acre, Eliot, Maine, August 1912

With a Group of Bahá'ís in
St. Paul, Minnesota, September 1912

On a Street in Kenosha, Wisconsin,
September 15, 1912

With Children on the Steps of the Home of Helen S. Goodall,
Oakland, California, October 1912

16

California

'Abdu'l-Bahá arrived in San Francisco on Tuesday, October 1, and remained there, with side trips to Oakland, Palo Alto, and Los Angeles, until Friday, October 25. Outwardly, many of the scenes familiar in other cities repeated themselves, as crowds hovered about Him like moths attracted to a light. Inwardly, each individual experienced a satisfying of personal needs that, in one sense, could never be shared, and that, in another, needed to be shared. For in dealing with each individual 'Abdu'l-Bahá demonstrated a facet of what each person must become in his dealings with others. He raised every act to a universal level by showing that people must become spiritual beings, reacting spontaneously to their environment, as He did, because thoroughly imbued with Bahá'u'lláh's divine Teachings.

'Abdu'l-Bahá was greeted at the train station by Dr. D'Evelyn; Mr. and Mrs. Ralston, Mrs. Helen Goodall, Mrs. Ella Cooper, and other friends awaited Him at a house He had rented at 1815 California Street. The rooms on the first floor of the house were so arranged that large doors opened into adjoining rooms. The area could thus be made into one large room, and it remained crowded throughout most of 'Abdu'l-Bahá's stay. Upstairs,

'Abdu'l-Bahá held private interviews, and there He and His entourage had their rooms, 'Abdu'l-Bahá's corner room commanding an extensive view of the city.

The people who were attracted to 'Abdu'l-Bahá in San Francisco were as varied as ever. Each day the people in neighboring houses watched His comings and goings in the two automobiles sent by Mrs. Goodall, Mrs. Cooper, and the Ralstons for His drives. Newspaper reporters came, and a cross section of people, some returning to bring their children. Kanichi Yamamoto, the first Japanese Bahá'í, asked 'Abdu'l-Bahá to give Persian names to his three children. David Starr Jordan, the president of Leland Stanford Junior University, came; and the mayor of Berkeley asked questions concerning economics. On October 4, after an afternoon visit to Golden Gate Park, 'Abdu'l-Bahá sent one of His frequent telegrams to the Persian friends, informing them of the events of His historic journey. This time He reported, "'We are in utmost joy among the friends of San Francisco. The confirmations are really overwhelming and the happiness overflowing.'"

On His first Sunday in San Francisco, October 6, 'Abdu'l-Bahá addressed the congregation of the First Unitarian Church in the morning and of the First Congregational Church of Oakland in the evening. On Monday, at a meeting arranged by Mr. Yamamoto, He addressed the Japanese YMCA at the Japanese Independent Church in Oakland, the talk being translated first into English, and then into Japanese.[1] From that time on some of the Japanese inquirers were present in almost every gathering.

He spoke at Leland Stanford Junior University in Palo Alto on Tuesday, October 8, and lunched with President

Jordan at his home afterward. That evening He spoke at the Palo Alto Unitarian Church. An entire edition of the *Palo Altan* was devoted to articles concerning His visit and transcriptions of His addresses. The main headline of the November 1 edition read, "ABDUL BAHA, THE BAHA'I PROPHET, SPEAKS AT STANFORD UNIVERSITY." Among the various articles were the following reports:

> A crowded Assembly Hall, holding nearly two thousand people, awaited with eager expectancy the appearance last Tuesday morning, of Abdul Baha, Abbas Effendi, the world leader of the Bahai movement. . . .
>
> It [the Bahá'í Faith] is truly catholic. Christian and Jew, Moslem and Buddhist, are numbered among its adherents. Not a sect itself, it makes appeal to all the sects. Its ideal is the one God, the God of all the religions. Unity and universal concord: those are its aims and objects. . . .
>
> . . . Those who pray for the coming of the kingdom of God on earth may see in Abbas Effendi one who dwells in that kingdom consciously, and creates an environment pulsating with the peace that passeth ordinary understanding. . . .
>
> . . . Abbas Effendi leads his followers over what is elsewhere called the Mystic Way; but wherever they march, they tread with practical feet. . . .

On Wednesday, October 9, 'Abdu'l-Bahá spoke to a large gathering at a high school auditorium in Berkeley. On October 10 He addressed the Open Forum in San Francisco and the next day spoke to the Theosophical

Society. On Saturday, October 12, He presented His memorable address to an audience of 2,000 in the Temple Emmanu-El, emphasizing "the truth of His Holiness Christ, the reality of Islam, the oneness of humanity and universal peace." On Sunday, October 13, He spoke at the reading room for the blind.

On Monday afternoon He went with the Persian friends to the estate of Phoebe Hearst, at her invitation, and remained for two nights. Maḥmúd observed, "Some of the relatives of the lady were also present. As there were people of different dispositions, the discourses of the Beloved were brief and full of wisdom according to the exigencies of the occasion. Many important ideas were couched in condensed sentences so that they made the maximum of effect with the minimum of words."

The next morning, in general conversation, the Presidential election was mentioned. "'The president,'" 'Abdu'l-Bahá noted, "'must be a man who is not hankering for the presidency. He should be a person free from all thoughts of name and fame; he must think himself unworthy of the rank; and should say that he thinks himself unfit for the place and unable to bear this burdensome duty. . . . If the public good is the object, the president must be a person sensitive to the public weal and not a selfish and self-seeking one.'" During the day 'Abdu'l-Bahá and the Persian friends toured the gardens. Before leaving on Wednesday morning, 'Abdu'l-Bahá called all the servants together, thanked them, and gave them ten dollars each.

After returning to San Francisco, He spoke at the Century Club concerning the rights of women. At the Nineteen Day Feast that evening, at the home of Mrs. Goodall in Oakland, 125 were present. The friends played the piano and sang before the meeting. Then 'Abdu'l-Bahá annointed each guest with attar of roses and served them Himself, speaking afterward of spiritual development. He remained in Oakland overnight. Early Thursday morning He returned to San Francisco. People came to talk with Him throughout the day.

On Friday, October 18, when friends from Seattle and Portland came to supplicate Him to visit Oregon and Washington, He replied, "'. . . tell them that I am always with them. Bodily meeting is nothing compared with spiritual connections.'"

Later that day 'Abdu'l-Bahá boarded the train for Los Angeles, taking with Him Mrs. Goodall, Mrs. Ralston, and the Persian friends. In Los Angeles, inquirers, reporters, and friends crowded around Him. To the many people seeking to arrange speaking engagements, He replied, "'I have no time. I have come here to see the tomb of Mr. Chase and to meet some friends.'" Thornton Chase, the first American to become a Bahá'í, had died on September 30, while 'Abdu'l-Bahá was enroute from Glenwood Springs, Colorado, to California.

On Saturday, October 19, after morning prayers, 'Abdu'l-Bahá, accompanied by several others, took the streetcar for the cemetery. There He went to the grave without asking its location. He chanted the Tablet of Visitation for Bahá'u'lláh and the Báb and a prayer for the departed and spoke briefly of the self-sacrifice and services rendered by Thornton Chase.[2] When He kissed the grave, tears came to the eyes of the onlookers.

The remainder of 'Abdu'l-Bahá's time in Los Angeles was packed with interviews, for throngs of people continued to seek Him out.

'Abdu'l-Bahá left Los Angeles Monday evening,

traveled all night, and arrived in San Francisco the next day. He then began preparations for the journey back across the country. But the crowds kept coming, and rounds of public meetings continued to the last moment. Immersing them in words and deeds that were the expressions of His love, He talked to them of spiritual growth, of teaching the Cause, of sowing the seeds. On His last day in San Francisco, Friday, October 25, 'Abdu'l-Bahá told them:

I have come to say good-bye. How grateful we should be to the Blessed Beauty who has created such affection in our hearts. This attar that I am sprinkling on you is a fragrance from the paradise of Abhá. . . . These days of meeting were days of happiness. . . . I beg of God to bring forth the results of these friendships so that they may become the Cause of enlightenment to the world and of guidance to all who live on earth.

Among the many newspaper articles which reported 'Abdu'l-Bahá's visits to San Francisco and Los Angeles were these:

San Francisco Examiner, October 7: ABDUL BAHA BRINGS GOSPEL OF PEACE.
. . . Abdul Baha, head of the Bahai religious movement, spoke at the First Unitarian Church, Franklin and Geary streets. . . . the venerable leader of the faith which now numbers more than three million followers looked like a patriarch of old as he stood in the pulpit and addressed the multitude in the church, on peace and love for all mankind.
San Francisco Monitor, October 5 editorial: BAHA.

. . . If Catholics should find themselves bitten by curiosity to look into these diabolical things, let them make the Sign of the Cross and pray that they be freed from temptation. They might say a prayer, too, for the silly deluded ones who have been caught in the net, that they be freed from their sins. For there are many of them. . . .

Keep away from Baha, no matter how beautifully his "gentle teachings" may be exploited during his stay in San Francisco. Don't go near him. Stay at home and say the Rosary instead.

Los Angeles Herald, October 19: NOTED PERSIAN IS HERE TO PLEAD FOR PEACE.

Abdul Baha Abbas . . . head of the great Bahai movement, a leader in the campaign for universal peace and a man whose teachings are read in every land, arrived in the city today to preach the gospel of universal peace. . . .

. . . Upon his arrival he immediately took quarters at the Hotel Lankershim. He had hardly become seated when the telephone began ringing and his followers came flocking in to see him.

This morning Abdul Baha announced that one of the causes for his visit here was to conduct a memorial service for Thornton Chase of 227 Rampart Boulevard, who up to the time of his death two weeks ago was one of the strongest followers of the Bahai movement on the Pacific coast. The ceremony took place this morning in Inglewood cemetery in the presence of several friends of the deceased.

'Abdu'l-Bahá left San Francisco by train on Friday morning, October 25, and arrived in Sacramento at noon.

He went to the home of Miss Christine Fraser but sent most of His entourage to the Hotel Sacramento. He said to her, "'You had a desire to call Me to your house. I have now come. I shall take My luncheon here, but for the night I wish to go to the hotel; for wherever I have gone I have stopped at hotels, notwithstanding the supplications of the friends to stay in their homes. I have not accepted their offer, but today I stopped at yours.'" After lunch, on the way to the hotel, He said, "'I desire to act always according to the counsel of the friends. But in matters expedient to the interest of the Cause of God, I do what I find useful to the Cause. The value of My practice and companionship is not known yet but it shall be known later.'"

A public meeting was held in the hotel that night, with such a response that another meeting was arranged at the same place for the following morning. At 1:00 P.M. on Saturday, October 26, He left Sacramento, for Denver.

17

The Journey East:
Teaching on the Train

During the pleasant journey from Sacramento to Denver, 'Abdu'l-Bahá related many stories to His five traveling companions. When the conductor and other railroad employees came through, they recalled that they had been on the same train with 'Abdu'l-Bahá on His journey going to San Francisco. 'Abdu'l-Bahá replied, "'Yes, it was so destined that I should see you once more on this trip.'"

When a salesman came through the cars selling pennants of various schools, 'Abdu'l-Bahá joked, "'Tell him to bring the banner of universal peace if he has it. We want a flag under which the whole world may find rest and peace.'" As other passengers heard Him speaking, they were attracted to Him and came from their seats to talk with Him. Finally a whole circle of people stood in the aisle around Him.

That night 'Abdu'l-Bahá again did not accept the suggestion that they get pullman accommodations, and He and His companions slept in the chair car. The next morning, Sunday, October 27, one of the ladies to whom He had spoken the day before came to say that she accepted the Teachings of Bahá'u'lláh. More people conversed with Him throughout the day. When one asked Him about His purpose for traveling in America, He replied:

I have come to America to raise the standard of universal peace and to bring unity among mankind. . . . But some persons ask questions about My country. Is it prosperous, and has it good trees, sweet fruits, pretty animals and lovely Arabian horses? Calling them to the Kingdom of God, I speak with them about the trees of the world of existence, the fruits of the human virtues, and the morals and traits of Heaven.

In the afternoon some of the train cars were attached to a section going to Salt Lake City, while the remaining cars, including that of 'Abdu'l-Bahá, were prepared for the trip to Denver. One woman tried to have her ticket changed from Salt Lake City so she could accompany 'Abdu'l-Bahá, but it was not possible. She asked where she could contact the Bahá'ís, and 'Abdu'l-Bahá gave her the address of some of the friends.

Again that night Maḥmúd and the others requested 'Abdu'l-Bahá's permission to secure pullman accommodations, and, again, He declined, preferring to sleep in the chair car.

The next day, October 28, after 'Abdu'l-Bahá had revealed Tablets in response to various communications, a salesman came through the car with little ore samples. As 'Abdu'l-Bahá looked at these, some children came up. He talked lovingly with them, and then bought each one of them a dollar's worth. Other children, seeing this, came running; 'Abdu'l-Bahá said jokingly, "'They, too, have come with beggars' looks!'" as He bought the same amount for each of them.

Observing His kindness, the parents and others came and began to ask Him questions, until, again, there was a crowd standing in the aisle and sitting on chair arms, as

He taught them of Bahá'u'lláh's Revelation. Maḥmúd noted, "We had never seen or heard the Cause taught in such a manner."

In the afternoon 'Abdu'l-Bahá ordered tea and soup for a large number of Turks who were en route home to take up arms in the Turkish-Greek conflict and talked with them of universal peace. When the train reached Denver at midnight, He got off and went to a hotel near the station.

The friends and reporters, hearing of His arrival, thronged to the hotel. On Tuesday 'Abdu'l-Bahá granted a succession of interviews and spoke to gatherings at the home of Mrs. Sidney Roberts, where He had spoken on His first visit to Denver, and at the Church of the Messiah. He and His companions then returned to the hotel, packed, and caught another train that evening. 'Abdu'l-Bahá said, "'We are going again toward the East. We have no more work in North America now.'"

Again He would not take pullman accommodations, even though requested by the friends, saying that they should not be dependent on bodily comforts: "'We must be equal to the hardships of traveling like a soldier in the path of Truth and not be slaves to bodily ease and comfort.'"

On the train the next day, October 30, 'Abdu'l-Bahá wrote an account of His travels in America, which, Maḥmúd noted, "are still among the papers of His personal belongings and have not as yet been published."

In the afternoon He began to talk with people in the seats nearby. After a few general remarks He began to discuss the Teachings, and again the people were attracted to come and cluster around Him to learn more.

That night there is no record of the little five-member

"army of God" that accompanied 'Abdu'l-Bahá requesting pullman accommodations. Perhaps they had finally accepted, after the months of travel, the lesson of "traveling like a soldier in the path of Truth." In any event 'Abdu'l-Bahá told them to reserve six berths for that night because too much austerity was not good. They suggested that perhaps only one might be secured for Him, and He replied, "'No, we must share equally.'"

At daybreak on Thursday, October 31, the train was approaching Chicago.

18

The Journey East: Chicago, Cincinnati, Washington, D.C., Baltimore

'Abdu'l-Bahá went again to the Plaza Hotel in Chicago, and the friends and inquirers again came in great numbers for interviews. He spoke in the evening to a large gathering in a hall of the hotel and the next day, Friday, November 1, continued to meet the crowds who sought Him.

He went with one man to view a private collection of ancient art and, on returning to the friends, said, "'This man took Me to his house to show pictures which are nothing more than the toys of children and they are ignorant of this marvel of divine strength.'"

At an interracial meeting on Saturday He said, "'A man who seeks piety is virtuous, whether he puts on a black garment or one of white.'" Later He went to Mrs. Corinne True's home where the friends were assembled for a "board of consultation" meeting and told them, "'The first duty of the members of such a board would be to have love and unity among themselves. If there is no unity and it turns out to be a cause of disunion, its non-existence is better.'"

The *Chicago Inter-Ocean*, on November 2, in an article titled "HEAD OF BAHAI RELIGION IN CHICAGO FOR LECTURES: Persian Prophet Urges World-Wide

Peace—Temple Planned for This City," noted:

> Abdul Baha Abbas, Persian prophet and head of the Bahai religion, arrived in Chicago yesterday for a series of three lectures on universal peace and to complete plans for the building of a Bahai temple near this city. The institution will be located in Wilmette and will consist of a school, hospital, church and an institute for the blind, to cost $50,000. Abdul Baha is making a tour of the United States, where he has many followers. He is accompanied by four of his countrymen and is staying at the Plaza hotel.
>
> He made an address at the Chicago Athletic association yesterday afternoon and urged that means be taken to establish world-wide peace. He spoke through His interpreter, Dr. Ameen Fareed. Abdul Baha is the son of the founder of Bahaism. He declares that he is not a prophet, but only a teacher. He explained that his mission is to teach international peace and a universal unity of religion and education.

On Sunday, November 3, along with a Sherlock Holmes serial story and advertisements for oleomargarine, the Chicago newspapers reported:

> U.S. Ready to Invade Cuba If Necessary
> Marriage of 'Isa' to Prince George to Be Annulled
> Germans Taking Lands of Poles Under New Law
> Big Hunger Strike Is Suffragist Plan
> Notre Dame Beats Pittsburgh

On Monday, November 4, the *Chicago Record-Herald* reported:

Abdul Baha Abbas, head of the oldest man-made universal peace movement, spoke in Chicago congregational churches yesterday. . . . In the afternoon he occupied Dr. Joseph A. Milburn's pulpit in Plymouth Church and in the morning he spoke at Pilgrim Church. With Abdul Baha Abbas was Dr. Ameen N. Fareed, who interpreted for him, and Mirza Ali Akbar, Mirza Ahmad Sohrab, Mirza Mahmood and Fugita. They have been touring the United States for eight months.

Before leaving Chicago that day, 'Abdu'l-Bahá sent a telegram to Cincinnati informing the friends, who had been supplicating His presence, that He would stay there for one night and that the stay would be "private." The friends met Him at the Cincinnati station and took Him to the Grand Hotel where a public meeting with five hundred persons attending had been arranged, followed by a banquet.

The next day the *Cincinnati Inquirer* reported that "Dr. Abdul Baha" had spoken. It also reported that Woodrow Wilson had been elected President of the United States.

'Abdu'l-Bahá's departure from Cincinnati was delayed until noon on November 5, because of the crowds that came to see Him. He went by train to Washington, D.C., where the *Evening Star* announced on Wednesday, November 6, that 'Abdu'l-Bahá "arrived in Washington from Cincinnati at 8:45 o'clock this morning."

The friends soon packed the house He had rented to hear about His journey to the West. He continued to talk with the friends during the next few days, and they strained to receive the final words from Him, knowing that soon He would depart. On Thursday He spoke at the Church of Brotherhood and on Friday, at a synagogue.

There He explained with force and clarity the unity of Judaism, Christianity, and Islám. At one point some persons sitting toward the front of the congregation made signs to the interpreter to indicate that the time was up. But 'Abdu'l-Bahá continued to speak.

Saturday night, November 9, the friends held a banquet at Rauscher's Hall. In the center of the room the tables were arranged in a figure nine and decorated with flowers. The walls were hung with flags, festoons, lanterns, and signs, with the Greatest Name above them. To the three hundred people at the banquet Mason Remey read a paper congratulating 'Abdu'l-Bahá and assuring Him of their obedience and renunciation. After they sang, 'Abdu'l-Bahá prayed and told everyone to begin eating. While they ate, He walked among them distributing candy and flowers and applying attar of roses. When He finished, the friends again sang songs. Then He spoke to them concerning the living of a Bahá'í life, and afterward they again burst into song.

When He returned to His rooms, many came requesting private interviews. Among them was a person who had lost both legs in a railroad accident and wore artificial limbs. 'Abdu'l-Bahá told him, "'Mutilation of the body brings no defect to the soul. This is one of the proofs of the immortality of the spirit, for death is another name for change and dispersion of the members and elements of the body.'" When the Consul General of Turkey and others came, He spoke to them about The Universal House of Justice.

On Sunday the entire day was occupied with interview after interview, until He went to the home of Mr. and Mrs. Joseph H. Hannen, 1252 Eighth Street, N.W., for a meeting. He looked at the interracial gathering and said:

This is a beautiful assembly. I am very happy that the whites and colored are together. This is the cause of my happiness, for you all are the servants of one God and therefore brothers, sisters, mothers and fathers. In the sight of God there is no distinction between white and colored; all are as one. Any one whose heart is pure is dear to God whether white or colored, red or yellow. . . .

Then He told them of Isfandiyár, a man of African ancestry, who served Bahá'u'lláh in Persia, before His exile:

If a perfect man could be found in the world, that man was Isfandyar. He was the essence of love, radiant with sanctity and perfection, luminous with light. Whenever I think of Isfandyar I am moved to tears although he passed away fifty years ago. He was the faithful servant of Baha'u'llah and was entrusted with his secrets. For this reason the shah of Persia wanted him and inquired continually as to his whereabouts. His Holiness Baha'u'llah was in prison but the shah had commanded many persons to find Isfandyar. . . . If they had succeeded in catching him they would not have killed him at once. They would have cut his flesh into pieces to force him to tell them the secrets of Baha'u'llah. But Isfandyar with the utmost dignity used to walk in the streets and bazaars. One day he came to us. My mother, my sister and myself lived in a house near a corner. . . . our enemies frequently injured us. . . . I was a child at that time. At midnight Isfandyar came in. My mother said, "O Isfandyar, there are a hundred policemen seeking for you. If they catch you they will not kill you at once but will torture you with fire. They will cut off your fingers. They will cut off your ears. They will put out your eyes to force you to tell them the secrets of Baha'u'llah. Go away! Do not stay here." He said "I cannot go, because I owe money in the street and in the stores. How can I go? They will say that the servant of Baha'u'llah has bought and consumed goods and sup-plies of the storekeepers without paying for them. . . . But if they take me, never mind. If they punish me, there is no harm in that. If they kill me, do not be grieved. But to go away is impossible. . . ." Isfandyar went about in the streets and bazaars. He had things to sell and from his earnings he gradually paid his cred-itors. In fact they were not his debts but the debts of the court, for all our properties had been confiscated. Eve-rything we had was taken away from us. The only things that remained were our debts. Isfandyar paid them in full; not a single penny remained unpaid. . . . his color was black, yet his character was luminous, his mind was luminous, his face was luminous. Truly he was a point of light.

. . . it is evident that excellence does not depend upon color. Character is the true criterion of humanity. Anyone who possesses a good character, who has faith in God and is firm, whose actions are good, whose speech is good,—that one is accepted at the threshold of God no matter what color he may be. In short—praise be to God!—you are the servants of God. The love of Baha'u'llah is in your hearts. Your souls are rejoicing in the glad-tidings of Baha'u'llah. My hope is that the white and the colored will be united in perfect love and fellowship, with complete unity and brotherhood. As-sociate with each other, think of each other and be like a rose-garden. Anyone who goes into a rose-garden will see various roses, white, pink, yellow, red, all growing together and replete with adornment. Each one accentuates the beauty of the other. . . . Although different in colors, yet—praise be to God!—you receive rays from the same sun. From one cloud the rain is poured upon you. You are under the training of one gardener and this gardener is kind to all. Therefore you must manifest the utmost kindness towards each other and you may rest assured that whenever you are united, the confirmations of the kingdom of Abha will reach you, the heavenly favors will descend, the bounties of God will be bestowed, the Sun of Reality will shine, the cloud of mercy will pour its showers and the breeze of divine generosity will waft its fragrances upon you.

. . . How beautiful to see colored and white together! I hope, God willing, the day may come when I shall see the red men, the Indians with you, also Japanese and others. Then there will be white roses, yellow roses, red roses and a very wonderful rose-garden will appear in the world.[1]

'Abdu'l-Bahá traveled to Baltimore on Monday, November 11, went to a hotel, granted interviews to the press, spoke at a Unitarian Church, and went for a late breakfast at the Struvens' home.

He wired the friends in Philadelphia, who had been asking Him to come, that His train would be passing through their city and that He would see them at the station. They were on the platform when He arrived and rushed joyously to Him. Most got on the train and rode with Him to the next station. They were joyful, en-

thusiastic, and departed weeping, a sight which so amazed
the other people on the train that they came to find out
who these people were. 'Abdu'l-Bahá talked to them and,
at their request, gave them the addresses of Bahá'ís whom
they could ask for further information.

19

Final Days in America:
New York City

Back, at last, in New York, for His final weeks in America, 'Abdu'l-Bahá rented the same house as before on Riverside Drive near the Hudson River; Maḥmúd noted, on November 11, "The owner of the house and his relatives had entered the group of the sincere ones. . . ."

From November 12 until December 5 'Abdu'l-Bahá stayed in New York and could be said to have conducted a month-long deepening class on every aspect of the Faith. Although invitations to speak poured in, He now refused most of them, for He preferred instead to visit the homes of the friends or to have them come to His house. Day and night, in this last face-to-face effort, He prepared them, as part of the army of God, for the things they must do, for the sacrifices they must make, for the spirituality they must attain, for the lessons they must learn, for the total integration and oneness they must achieve, and for the service they would be called upon to render to their fellowmen in the path of Bahá'u'lláh.

To know the events of these days fully would be to know the weaving in and out of each human experience, as each person emerged from all his past experiences, entered 'Abdu'l-Bahá's presence, and went again into the world. To see how the fabric of the new World Order was being woven, in that rented house on Riverside Drive, those thousands of threads, along with their effects on other lives, would have to be followed from beginning to end.

On November 12 Maḥmúd recorded that the newspapers were filled with accounts of the war between the Balkan States and Turkey. He added, "the people looked upon us with eyes full of prejudice whenever they saw us in the market in Persian gowns. We were even refused accommodation in large hotels as they thought we were Turks."

On the same day he recorded that 'Abdu'l-Bahá, as before, was invited to the homes of many socially prominent New Yorkers. But 'Abdu'l-Bahá refused, saying, "'I have work with the poor and not with the rich. I love all with heart and soul yet I am not here to visit the homes of the rich.'" When Andrew Carnegie implored Him to come, however, He did bestow upon him the honor of His presence. On November 19 the *New York Times*, in an article entitled "PROPHET BLESSES MORGAN," reported:

J. Pierpont Morgan was written down yesterday as one who had done "considerable philanthropy" when his library in East Thirty-sixth Street was visited by Abdul Baha, the Persian prophet. After the patriarch had wandered through the treasure rooms, he paused before the album long enough to write a blessing on the financier and thereto append his autograph. Beneath the Persian script his companion, Dr. Ameen Fareed, wrote this translation:

O, Thou Generous Lord, verily this famous personage has done considerable philanthropy, render him great and dear in Thy Kingdom, make him happy and joyous in both worlds, and confirm him in serving the Oneness, the world of humanity, and submerge him in the sea of Thy Favors.

ABDUL BAHA ABBAS

One of the few speaking invitations 'Abdu'l-Bahá accepted was that, on November 15, to address the Divine Knowledge Club, comprised mostly of women, the leader of whom claimed clairvoyance and sat with her eyes closed most of the time to receive inspiration. On the way home, 'Abdu'l-Bahá said, "'Behold: what superstition and vain thoughts are yet prevalent in America!'"

On November 19 Maḥmúd noted, "A number of school children gathered near the Beloved saying, 'Who is this person who looks like Christ?' Miss Juliet Thompson spoke to them outside the house about the Beloved Cause and the life of 'Abdu'l-Bahá. They asked to interview Him and they were invited to come. . . ."

The days of 'Abdu'l-Bahá's visit were passing quickly. A farewell banquet was planned on November 23 at the Great Northern Hotel, where Howard Colby Ives estimated there were six hundred, and Maḥmúd, three hundred, present. The banquet hall was regal with festoons, banners, and flowers, the crystal glistening beneath the lights. The Master spoke of the oneness of mankind to the white Bahá'ís. The next night, at the Kinneys', 'Abdu'l-Bahá and the white friends served the black friends whom the hotel management had vehemently excluded the night before. 'Abdu'l-Bahá said, "'Today you have shown the Commandments of the Blessed Beauty in your actions and have acted according to the teachings of the Supreme Pen.'"

The *New York Tribune*, on November 24, in an article headed "ABDUL BAHA GOING AWAY," noted:

Abdul Baha, Abbas Effendi, the Persian prophet and center of the Bahai movement, received assurances of unswerving loyalty last night from members of the Bahai assembly of New York City, who gathered at a farewell dinner in his honor at the Great Northern Hotel. The Oriental savant is to leave this country this week, presumably on the steamship Mauretania, though none of his followers would venture to make a definite date, as Abdul Baha, they said, made his plans from day to day.

The hour of the farewell dinner was unusually late. At precisely 9:40 o'clock Abdul Baha appeared, a venerable figure, with a long gray beard and a Persian cloak and white turban, walking slowly to his place of honor.

. . . He was received with a silent greeting by the three hundred members of the assembly, who rose at his approach.

On November 25 the crowds kept coming to see Him. Maḥmúd noted, "As the multitude grew He could not conveniently see them individually so He came down stairs to apologize for not being able to see them."

On November 26 the *New York Tribune* reported:

Mrs. Mary Stokes MacNutt, President of Minerva, and Mr. MacNutt were a happy pair yesterday, for they got Abdul Baha, of Persia, to speak at the club's annual luncheon at the Waldorf-Astoria.

. . . he came . . . looking as if he had on the same white turban and the same long gown that he wore when he landed here from Persia last April.

His face was just as peaceful as it was then, too . . .
and he didn't seem the least bit touched by his seven
months of America. . . .

On Wednesday, November 27, during His discourses
throughout the day, He told His listeners at one point,
"'Their [the Manifestations'] only motive was the education of blessed souls and sanctified spirits who became the
teachers of the divine education and the promoters of the
Great Guidance and the Supreme Favor. The people of
Bahá must endeavor day and night to enforce this noble
purpose. They must put forth their energy to educate
themselves and other sanctified souls.'"

On November 28, Thanksgiving Day, Maḥmúd commented:

During these last days of His stay in America, there
was always an influx of friends in His Presence. They
came to offer supplications, to turn to the eternal Face,
to look upon the Dawning Place of the Divine Covenant, and to cling to His Mantle of Favor. Every moment
the cries of the lovers increased and the fire of love in the
breasts glowed more. There was not a moment's rest for
the Holy Being. He was either delivering an address to
a public meeting or talking to a friend in His private
chamber. The Holy Tongue was imparting joy to the
sad, hope to the hopeless, and a flame to the dormant
while He guided strugglers to the Right Path.

On Friday, November 29, He moved to the Emery
home. In an evening meeting at the Kinneys', He spoke
with the friends about their offers of money. He said,
"'Distribute it among the poor from Me. It will be as if I

have given it to them. The most acceptable offering to Me is the unity among friends, service to the Cause of God, diffusing the Divine Fragrances, and acting upon the admonitions of the Beauty of Abhá.'"

The friends kept trying to give Him money, supplicating by letter and in person, asking the Persians to intercede. Finally, on November 30, some devised a plan for clinging to His mantle until He would accept it. He called in others and said to them all:

> I am pleased with your services and I am grateful for all you have done for Me. . . . Now you have brought presents for the members of My family. They are acceptable, but the best of all presents is the love of God which remains preserved in the treasuries of hearts. Material presents remain for a time but this lasts forever. These presents require chests and shelves for safekeeping while this is preserved in the repositories of the minds and hearts and remains eternal and immortal forever in the divine worlds. I shall, therefore, convey to them your love which is the most precious of all gifts. No one uses diamond rings in our home and no one wants rubies. That house is free from all these things.
>
> I, however, accept your presents but I leave them in your safe keeping with the request that you will kindly sell them and send the proceeds to the funds for the Mashriqu'l-Adhkár. . . .

On Sunday, December 1, one of the subjects 'Abdu'l-Bahá discussed was universal peace:

> . . . they [Americans] can succeed in bringing about universal peace, provided they take the right stand and

the nation and government put forth strenuous efforts to carry out the teaching and principles of God. This question of peace in the religion of Bahá'u'lláh is a positive command and religious obligation. It is not the resolution of a congress or the edict of a parliament of a nation or a country so that it can be considered as permeated with selfish desires and be subject to amendments. It is a positive divine command and is, thus, certain to come to pass. As opposition to Christ is considered a sin in the terminology of that religion, the rejection of peace has the same status in the religion of Bahá'u'lláh.

It was on Monday, December 2—the day the newspapers announced Sarah Bernhardt's arrival in New York to start a vaudeville tour—that 'Abdu'l-Bahá summed up how the friends must be:

> These are the days of my farewell to you for I am sailing on the fifth of the month. . . . I must therefore give you my instructions and exhortations today and these are none other than the teachings of Bahá'u'lláh.
> You must manifest complete love and affection toward all mankind. Do not exalt yourselves above others but consider all as your equals, recognizing them as the servants of one God. Know that God is compassionate toward all; therefore love all from the depths of your hearts, prefer all religionists before yourselves, be filled with love for every race and be kind toward the people of all nationalities. Never speak disparagingly of others but praise without distinction. Pollute not your tongues by speaking evil of another. Recognize your enemies as friends and consider those who wish you evil as the

wishers of good. You must not see evil as evil and then compromise with your opinion, for to treat in a smooth kindly way one whom you consider evil or an enemy, is hypocrisy and this is not worthy or allowable. You must consider your enemies as your friends, look upon your evil-wishers as your well-wishers and treat them accordingly. Act in such a way that your heart may be free from hatred. Let not your heart be offended with anyone. If some one commits an error and wrong toward you, you must instantly forgive him. Do not complain of others. Refrain from reprimanding them and if you wish to give admonition or advice let it be offered in such a way that it will not burden the bearer. Turn all your thoughts toward bringing joy to hearts. Beware! Beware! lest ye offend any heart. Assist the world of humanity as much as possible. Be the source of consolation to every sad one, assist every weak one, be helpful to every indigent one, care for every sick one, be the cause of glorification to every lowly one and shelter those who are overshadowed by fear.

In brief, let each one of you be as a lamp shining forth with the light of the virtues of the world of humanity. Be trustworthy, sincere, affectionate and replete with chastity. Be illumined, be spiritual, be divine, be glorious, be quickened of God, be a Baha'i.[1]

Maḥmúd noted on December 3:

Today a spirit of sadness came over the lovers of the Peerless Beauty as preparations were made for His leaving.

Two well attended meetings were held—one in the

afternoon at the home of Mrs. Krug, and the other at the home of Mrs. Kinney.

On December 4 'Abdu'l-Bahá continued to talk with the streams of visitors. That night He addressed the Theosophical Society of New York, saying in conclusion:

> For nine months I have been touring in America, calling the people to the oneness of humanity. I have delivered addresses in large churches and worshiping places of many cities, having invited the people to the love and unity of mankind. . . .
> Since I shall leave your shores tomorrow, I bid you good-bye. I pray that divine confirmations, heavenly honor, and eternal life be given to you so that you may reach the highest station of the world of man. I am grateful to you and shall never forget you. I shall ever supplicate to the Court of God and beg divine assistance and heavenly bounty for you.

Finally, Thursday, December 5, the day of departure from America, came. Two hundred thirty-nine days had passed while 'Abdu'l-Bahá traveled across the North American continent, from the Atlantic to the Pacific, proclaiming Bahá'u'lláh's Message for a new Era, promulgating universal peace, communicating to the hearts, opening spiritual eyes and ears and minds, deepening the friends, with little rest, in railway cars, assembly halls, His private rooms, the homes of the friends, and glittering embassies. He had cut across the forms and fetters of social class, race, and color. He had talked to university students and Bowery inhabitants; attended a Broadway play; toured the Hearst estate; and conversed with former President Theodore Roosevelt, inventor Alexander Graham Bell, and politicians, scientists, industrialists, and clergymen. He had chided reporters and joked with admirals and Supreme Court Justices; had spoken of Christ in synagogues and of Muḥammad in churches; had been picketed at a meeting and evicted from His home; had refused lavish gifts; had bestowed tokens of wealth on the poor; had maintained an incredible flow of correspondence; and had notified repressed brethren in the East of victories in the West. He had loved the friends and disciplined them; had been gentle and firm; had walked with them through parks and a zoo; and had ridden in their cars and on streetcars and trains; and, as He gazed on green valleys, towering mountains, and rushing rivers, had called to memory the Blessed Perfection. He had uplifted, praised, and encouraged every sign of spiritual development shown by each soul.

In His autumn years that recalled a spring when there had been no classroom but the prison cell and the home of exile and no teacher but His Father, He had amazed experts in a variety of fields with His sagacity and wisdom. The Teachings of the perfect Instructor Bahá'u'lláh—a thousand or thousands of years of spiritual potential for the planet channeled into that single human form—were reflected in 'Abdu'l-Bahá, the perfect Pupil, the kind and simple, the saintly, the single-minded, laughing, enduring mystery of a Man, Who had been appointed by that same Instructor as the pivot of the Covenant of God with all the earth. He performed in each small action the seed-planting for a millenium. The Exemplar, the Master, the Servant was now to leave the shores of America and return to the Threshold of the Holy Tomb of

Bahá'u'lláh to serve out His remaining years on earth. All the future, all the coming ages, all the children yet unborn would be dependent on the spiritual threads He had woven during His journeys across this and other lands. Not one breath would be drawn in the future centuries, not one word spoken or deed performed in that earth-wide, centuries-long tapestry of the World Order of Bahá'u'lláh, whose strands would not ultimately reach back to the Divine Loom of 'Abdu'l-Bahá, the Center of the Covenant.

The friends were already looking back, as they would increasingly in the future, on the rich store of experiences that had been woven together and were recounting their memories and recalling the interviews, articles, and news stories that had packed the eight and one-half months.

They could recall how some of the friends, in the infancy of their development, had been apprehensive about His coming to America, which had caused Muḥammad Yazdí to write these prophetic words from Egypt in 1911 to the American Bahá'ís:

> Some people have expressed anxieties and fears because of Abdul-Baha's possible visit to America; they think that the newspapers will write sensational articles and ridicule the Cause. Such people are very short-sighted. They have not realized deeply, nor superficially, the force of Abdul-Baha's presence. Neither have they dreamed of the magnetic influence of his Highness. . . . He is a man whose very appearance will solve all the perplexed anxieties of the visionaries of disaster. . . . Should we be afraid to receive the One who is the source of all our inspiration and all our light? . . . Future historians will record the coming of

Abdul-Baha to America as a great and momentous event. Broaden your vision and look into the future, when the nations of America shall celebrate, from one end of the continent to the other, the anniversary of the day when Abdul-Baha set foot upon "the land of the brave and the free!" . . . He does not want your houses and palaces, but your hearts. Prepare your hearts, purify your hearts, cleanse your hearts, that he may find a place therein![2]

The American friends had also been concerned about 'Abdu'l-Bahá's monetary well-being and recalled:

When the Bahais of this country received word of his intended visit, the sum of eighteen thousand dollars was subscribed toward the expense of his journey. He was notified of this action and a part of the money forwarded to him by cable. He cabled in answer that the funds contributed by his friends could not be accepted, returned the money and instructed them to give their offering to the poor.[3]

They recalled His arrival, and the general acclamation accorded Him by the public and the press, and the rare attacks, such as the one airing the views of the Reverend Peter Z. Easton which appeared in the *New York City Sun* on April 21. Entitled "WARNS AMERICANS AGAINST ABDUL BAHA," the account stated:

The American visit of Abdul Baha, head of Bahaism, to the United States has aroused the ire of the Rev. Peter Z. Easton, who has been a missionary since 1873 at Tabriz, in northern Persia, and who is now in London. In speaking to THE SUN correspondent Mr. Easton, who is shortly to leave London for Persia, said:

"I am firmly convinced that strong utterances should be made to awaken American Christians to the truth of Abdul Baha's propaganda. Bahaism is not Christian, it is not Mohammedan; on the contrary it is essentially anti-Christian and anti-Mohammedan. . . . I greatly fear that this cult of Bahaism may find fruitful ground in the United States and I am anxious to raise my voice and urge Christians to crush it in its infancy.

"Last September I called on Abdul Baha . . . in London to tell me what was the creed, a new gospel or what. I found him a man of great affability and courtesy. . . .

"After some introductory conversation I asked him what his message was. . . .

"Instead of answering my question he turned the conversation into another channel. . . .

"It is a pantheistic, not a Christian, not even a Mohammedan movement. . . .

". . . It strikes at the basis of Christianity."

They could recall the praise and honor heaped on 'Abdu'l-Bahá and the touching and humorous episodes recorded in the articles printed about Him, such as the one that also appeared on April 21, in the magazine section of the *New York Times*. The reporter, after covering in detail her extensive interview with 'Abdu'l-Bahá, related what happened after she and the translator left His room:

In a minute the door had closed and the reporter stepped from Palestine to the conventional hotel sitting room. The interpreter was beside her.

"Is he not a kind man?" he asked, all his face aglow with affection for his master. "He is the kindest man in the world."

"Indeed, yes."

"You travel with him?"

"Yes, I interpret for him. . . ."

An American Bahai came up. His fashion of putting his devotion was somewhat in contrast to the Oriental way of speaking that had prevailed in the apartment, but it bore witness to the love the master inspires.

"For that man," he said, "I'd jump head first from a fifteenth-story window."

So it is with everybody who has come in contact with Abdul Baha. . . .

A faith that is lived must grow, and Bahaism spreads in India, in Africa, in Persia, in England and France, and in the United States. It is not easy to give up prejudices, but Bahais who have done so find that they are considerably happier without them.

"I used to wash my hands after shaking hands with a Christian," said a Mohammedan Bahai. "Now I want to shake hands with all the world."

They could recall the letters to the editor and the un-signed reader's note about 'Abdu'l-Bahá, two of which appeared in the *New York City Evening Globe* on April 22:

Sir: In reply to "S.T.'s" request for expressions of opinion about Abdul Baha, the Persian teacher, permit me to say I enjoyed greatly hearing to-day this eloquent visitor from the Orient. His message . . . gave me many inspiring suggestions. He has an impressive and interesting personality and a patriarchal and kindly manner, with a face somewhat sad, which is as it should be in one who brings so noble a message and such a Christ-like appeal for world peace and friendship, regardless of creed or sect. . . . I felt . . . that this pilgrim from a far country was a master of the things of the spirit. . . .

Abdul Baha Abbas, now in New York to spread his gospel of peace, is found in Gertrude Atherton's new novel, "Julia France and Her Times," which the Macmillan Company has just published. The heroine of Mrs. Atherton's story . . . goes to Persia. "Even a little of the wisdom of the east," as she explains, "must widen our vision and prove an everlasting antidote to the modern spirit of unrest." She goes to Acca. And what took her to Acca?

"I went to see Abdul Baha Abbas and investigate the new religion. . . ."

Another letter to the editor was printed on April 29 in the *New York Evening Mail*:

Sir—You are surely correct in your editorial on Abdul Baha when you state that the world generally laughs at people with ideas, but after laughing long enough "turns around and eats the idea . . . ," only generally it changes the name of the idea and takes the credit for it.

The idea of Abdul Baha that all religions are one, based on identical truths . . . is a sublime conception . . . like very big things, seems almost too simple to be accomplished. Yet those who have heard Abdul Baha speak, who have heard his earnest plea for perfect tolerance, perfect co-operation in religious and other matters, must carry away in their hearts a high resolve to break down all barriers to human brotherhood. . . .

The friends could recall the magazine articles introducing information on the new religion. One appeared in the "Personals" section of the April 27 issue of *The Survey* magazine:

Wherever a Bahai center has been formed, there has been a new spirit and a new impetus to progress. Thirty years ago a book called the Mysterious Forces of Civilization, by a Bahai Philosopher, had a commanding influence in educating toward constitutional government in Persia. In recent developments, one of Shuster's chief supports were the women of Persia, who are coming out of their ignorance and seclusion through the teaching and example of the Bahai monogamous homes in their midst. . . . Bahais do not label as theirs the schools and hospitals they establish. But they are back of or within every progressive movement. They are responsible for the Persian-American Educational Society, the Orient-Occident Unity Society, and the Tarbiat Schools for both boys and girls in Teheran, Persia. American men and women are quietly going out into Bahai oriental centers, carrying education and the message of freedom. Their influence goes far because they become one with their surroundings and have no missionary label. . . . Bahais by thousands, unlabelled, are pushing the various peace organizations of different countries.

. . . Scientists and men of affairs who have met him ['Abdu'l-Bahá] marvel at his wisdom and common-sense knowledge of world conditions, questioning how he can meet them on their own level when he has been a political prisoner for forty years.[4]

They could remember how often the newspapers reported the superficial instead of the deep spiritual message, as in the May 14 article (picked up from a New York paper) in the *Chicago Record-Herald* headed "'ALL RIGHT,' NATION'S SLOGAN":

Abdul Baha, Persian prophet of world's peace, said today he had found the keynote expression of American optimism.

"It is those two words, 'all right,'" he said. "Everywhere I go," the Persian went on, "I hear those two magical words—words which I have never heard used by any other nation in any other country. With you Americans it is always 'all right.'"

"If I ask a bellboy at the hotel to do something, he responds, 'all right.' If I inquire as to the health of a person I have met here, he answers, 'all right.'"

"When the conductor wants the train to start, he shouts, 'all right.'"

"Everything is 'all right' in the United States. I believe the expression typically reflects the optimism of this great country."

The friends encountered articles in newspapers in many parts of the country before 'Abdu'l-Bahá visited there, or in places He never visited. The Wilmington,

Delaware, *Star* reported on June 30, in bold type above a long article on 'Abdu'l-Bahá:

> After forty years spent within the walls of a Turkish prison, Abbas Effendi, known to His thousands of followers as Abdul Baha, the Servant of God, has come to this country as the standard bearer of a new faith. To war with selfishness, to do away with prejudice, to proclaim the doctrine of universal brotherhood—these are the lessons that Abdul Baha teaches. Prejudices of nationality, of race, of religion—all these are a hindrance to the love of God and of man and should be forgotten. To be a Bahai is to be a little brother of all the world.

The *Los Angeles Times*, on June 19, four months before 'Abdu'l-Bahá's visit to California, reported:

> Several of the magazines are printing photographs of Abdul Baha and are paying some attention to his visit at this time to the United States. He is described by one of them as a man of loving kindness, spiritual breadth. . . . It is quite probable that Abdul Baha speaks far better for himself than others have spoken for him, and that his visit to America will be a help to the people here in a general way, quite regardless of its effect on the Bahaist movement. It is likely, too, that the practical application of this movement belongs more properly toward unifying the many sects of the Orient, but the unity of religious doctrine and purpose is a consummation to be striven for in all places.

Many small instances would be remembered and retold

by those who witnessed them. William Copeland Dodge recalled, for example, this glimpse:

> The homes of many of the believers were also visited by Abdul Baha. Among them was the residence of my mother and father at 261 West 139th Street, New York City, and my home, 1043 East 16th Street, Flatbush, Brooklyn.
>
> Abdul Baha had luncheon with us. We had placed a large, comfortable chair at the table for Him, but He sat in a smaller chair. Another example of humility![5]

Some people could not recall the specific things that went on in His presence but could remember the impact of His presence, as did Lucy Jane Marshall, who said of one meeting in California: "If he spoke or if anyone else was there, I do not recall; but O, in quiet times, the power of his presence, the peace in his face, and his steadfast eyes are with me still."[6]

Echoing in their memories, louder than all the words which others had spoken or written about Him, were the life-giving words of 'Abdu'l-Bahá Himself, over and over, by day and by night, privately and in groups—words rich in their truth and consistency, moving in their emotional impact, penetrating in their analysis, electrifying in the spiritual vistas they revealed, words He had used to train responsive souls to be able to serve the Cause of Bahá'u'lláh. Sometimes He trained them indirectly and sometimes directly, as when He said to them:

> I wish to train you until you have no other thought, no other motive, no other wish than service in the Cause of Bahá'o'lláh. The Divine Educators who have

brought the Light of Guidance to this world found neither rest nor comfort by day or night. Abraham, Moses, Jesus, Mohammed, Baha'o'llah—all the Heavenly Messengers suffered the utmost privation and underwent extreme hardships in the Pathway of God. They were exiled from their native land, imprisoned, driven from city to city; they were homeless, hungry and found no rest; they lived in the fields and hid in caves among the mountains; the sky was their canopy, the hard earth their bed. But all these difficulties and hardships served only to increase their power and accomplishment. . . .

It was so likewise with their disciples and followers. . . .

Through my training you must become so fitted to spread the Glad-Tidings of the Abha Kingdom that you will follow in the footsteps of these blessed ones in gladness. In Persia there is a wonderful breed of horses which are trained to run long distances at very great speed. They are most carefully trained at first. They are taken out into the fields and made to run a short course. At the commencement of their training they are not able to run far. The distance is gradually increased. They become thinner and thinner, wiry and lean, but their strength increases. Finally, after months of rigid training, their swiftness and endurance become wonderful. They are able to run at full speed across rough country many parasangs of distance. At first this would have been impossible. Not until they become trained, thin and wiry, can they endure this severe test.

In this way I shall train you. . . . (little by little, little by little), until your powers of endurance become so increased that you will serve the Cause of God continu-

ally, without other motive, without other thought or
wish. This is my desire.

You must become impervious to criticism, unconscious of attack and abuse, nay, rather welcoming persecution, hostility and bitterness as the means of testing
and increasing your supreme faith in God; even as His
Holiness Christ instructed His disciples, "Bless them
that curse you; pray for them that despitefully use
you." Be therefore as spiritual adamant against these
darts, arrows and swords of infliction. We will help
each other to bear them. First by love and increased zeal
in the Heavenly Cause. For by exercise the spirit grows
stronger, more capable of withstanding, just as the
muscle of the outer body increases its fibre through
continual action. You must help me and I will help you
to increase our service in the Cause of Baha'o'llah.
Secondly, we will help each other grow more and more
accustomed to punishment and persecution. Years ago
in Baghdad the usual punishment for offenders and
lawbreakers was the bastinado. The governor noticed
that a certain band of men came repeatedly before him
for trial. They were regularly found guilty of breaking
the law, sentenced and whipped upon the feet. While
the bastinado was being inflicted they appeared quite
comfortable and evidently unconscious of pain. In a few
days these same offenders would be back again, going
through the same process. The governor made careful
inquiry about them. It was learned that they lived
together in a house and that every day it was their
custom to bastinado each other until the skin upon their
feet had become so hardened to the whip that the legal
bastinado gave them no inconvenience whatever.

Now we, as offenders against the opinions of our

friends and enemies, must assist each other to become impervious to their criticism, unconscious of attack, welcoming their whips. You must beat me and I will beat you with the whips of love. The more we beat each other the more capable of withstanding we will become. When the enemies find they are increasing our love, enkindlement and service in the pathway of Baha'o'llah, they will wonder and say, "How is this? Our words have no effect upon them except to make them love us more and give thanks to God for our scourging."

The Blessed Beauty Baha'o'llah won the hearts of His jailers and tormentors. No one could withstand Him. The intense flame of His love melted the hardest stone of hearts. The more chains of iron they put upon His body, the more He imprisoned them in chains of love. They looked upon Him in wonder; they became His followers. [7]

Some of the friends could recall their desire after once meeting with Him to follow wherever He went. Mrs. Bertha Rohr Clark remembered:

At the Kinney home there were between three and four hundred souls waiting to receive His blessing. He came to each one of us and took our hands in His with a loving greeting and a few words I did not understand. However I felt an electric shock that went from my head to my feet. This was a day I am sure that no one that was present will ever forget. Whenever the Master spoke, in homes or churches, hall or societies, I went almost at the cost of my position which I [had] held for many years. [8]

Mrs. Hazel Tomlinson remembered:

. . . at His home, He asked to see me. When I went to Him, Ella Bailey was there also. . . .

While we were sitting there a bride and groom came in dressed in all their finery. She was white and he was colored. They knelt at Abdu'l-Baha's feet and He blessed them and put a candy in each mouth, saying as He did so, "The East and the West."

Then when we rose to go Abdu'l-Baha gave my sister (Kathryn Frankland) a banana and to me He gave a beautiful persimmon, my first one. It was delicious. Ever since then I have eaten many of them. . . .

I remember at one time in His home on California street. . . . There were a number of people around Him and a few reporters. He had given these reporters some very lovely roses with very long stems. They looked as if they didn't know what to do with them. . . .

Did we not always learn a lesson when with the Master? Even for a very few minutes while with Him. We scarcely knew how very important these minutes were to us and the whole world in general. . . . One evening He told us of the terrible Black pit where Baha'u'llah was confined for four months. . . . He was sitting on a low davenport. He said, "I was a child of eight," and He wept. He continued—"They had taken me to see Baha'u'llah when He would come out of this awful pit for a little fresh air and water. He was chained with convicts and murderers and His clothes were worn so thin and ragged, and He said, "'Why is this child here, take him away,' and they took me away." And the

Master still wept and we all wept with Him. Then He continued: "In all your Feasts and all your Meetings speak of Baha'u'llah and all His sufferings."[9]

The threads that He had woven would be traced and followed through the fabric of the World Order for the whole of a Dispensation.

And so it was, on December 5, 1912, on the 239th day after His arrival in America, 'Abdu'l-Bahá stood on the ship, *Celtic*, and looked at the friends, on whose actions, together with the actions of their fellow-believers, in large part hung the fate of the world. He said to them:

This is my last meeting with you, for now I am on the ship ready to sail away. These are my final words of exhortation. I have repeatedly summoned you to the cause of the unity of the world of humanity. . . .

The earth is one nativity, one home, and all mankind are the children of one father. . . . The obstacle to human happiness is racial or religious prejudice, the competitive struggle for existence and inhumanity toward each other.

Your eyes have been illumined, your ears are attentive, your hearts knowing. You must be free from prejudice and fanaticism, beholding no differences between the races and religions. . . . the best way to thank God is to love one another.

Beware lest ye offend any heart, lest ye speak against any one in his absence, lest ye estrange yourselves from the servants of God. . . .

. . . A world-enkindling fire is astir in the Balkans. God has created men to love each other, but instead, they kill each other with cruelty and bloodshed. . . .

As to you;—your efforts must be lofty. Exert yourselves with heart and soul so that perchance through your
efforts the light of Universal Peace may shine. . . .

Consider how the prophets who have been sent . . .
have exhorted mankind to unity and love. . . . Consider the heedlessness of the world . . . Notwithstanding the heavenly commandments to love one another,
they are still shedding each other's blood. . . .

Your duty is of another kind, for you are informed of
the mysteries of God. Your eyes are illumined, your
ears are quickened with hearing. You must therefore
look toward each other and then toward mankind with
the utmost love and kindness. You have no excuse to
bring before God if you fail to live according to his
command, for you are informed of that which consti-
tutes the good-pleasure of God. . . . It is my hope that
you may become successful in this high calling. . . .
And unto this I call you, praying to God to strengthen
and bless you.[10]

Notes

Notes

In order that excessive notes might not hinder the flow of the narrative, references have not been used when material from the diaries of Juliet Thompson and Maḥmúd-i Zarqání appears with the date and the author's name. The source of unidentified quotations is Maḥmúd's diary under the date being discussed. Entries in the diary from June 7 to August 10, however, are dated one day earlier than other Western sources date them. Dates from September 1 through October 3 are subject to further clarification. Establishing the dates of every episode in 'Abdu'l-Bahá's journey in America is difficult. Many can be verified by a number of sources; others cannot be so clearly and easily established. It will be the work of future historians to clarify the dates of 'Abdu'l-Bahá's entire itinerary in America.

Preface

1. Elbert Hubbard, "A Modern Prophet," *Hearst's Magazine*, 22 (July-Dec. 1912), 51.

2. 'Abdu'l-Bahá, *The Promulgation of Universal Peace: Discourses by Abdul Baha Abbas during His Visit to the United States in 1912*, [rev. ed.] in 1 vol. (Wilmette, Ill.: Bahai Publishing Committee, 1943), p. 1.

Chapter 1

1. Henry H. Jessup, "Religious Mission of the English Speaking Nations," in *The World's Parliament of Religions*, ed. John Henry Barrows, 2 vols. (Chicago: The Parliament Publishing Company, 1893), II, 1125–26.

2. Abdul-Baha Abbas, "Tablet to the American Friends from Abdul-Baha," *Star of the West*, 2, no. 4 (May 17, 1911), 6–7.

3. Edward G. Browne, trans., *A Traveller's Narrative* (New York: Baha'i Publishing Committee, 1930), p. xxxvi.

4. Ethel Stefana Stevens, "The Light in the Lantern," *Everybody's Magazine*, 25 (Dec. 1911), 779–82, 786.

5. "Abdul-Baha in Egypt," *Star of the West*, 1, no. 12 (Oct. 16, 1910), 1.

6. Quotations from Maḥmúd's diary are from an unpublished English translation that has long circulated among American Bahá'ís. The diary entitled *Badáyi'u'l-Áthár* (The Wondrous Annals) was published in Persian in Bombay, India, the first volume appearing in 1914, the second, in 1921. The following "Compiler's Note" appeared on the last page: "He [Maḥmúd] wrote it with his own hand, and submitted it in . . . [1913 to] 'Abdu'l-Bahá. . . . In the beginning of 1914 he was commanded to go to India and to publish the book. Thanks are due to his spiritual friends, Jináb Jawánmard Gushtásb and Mihtar Isfandiyár Bahrám, who defrayed the expenses of printing the book in the same year in Bombay, India." The house style of capitalization and of the transliteration of Persian and Arabic words has been used.

7. 'Abdu'l-Bahá, *Promulgation*, p. i.

Chapter 2

1. Wendell Phillips Dodge, "Abdul-Baha's Arrival in America," *Star of the West*, 3, no. 3 (Apr. 28, 1912), 3–5.

2. Edward B. Kinney was given the name *Ṣafá* ("purity") by 'Abdu'l-Bahá; his wife was called *Vafá* ("faithfulness").

3. 'Abdu'l-Bahá, *Promulgation*, p. 1.

4. Dodge, "Abdul-Baha's Arrival in America," p. 3.

5. Howard Colby Ives, *Portals to Freedom*, rev. ed. (London: George Ronald, 1962), p. 33.

6. 'Abdu'l-Bahá, *Promulgation*, p. 5.

7. Ibid., pp. 6–7.

8. Howard MacNutt, "Interview at Hotel Ansonia, New York City, April 13, 1912. —Abdul-Baha, Rev. J. T. Bixby and Rev. Howard Colby Ives, Present," *Star of the West*, 3, no. 8 (Aug. 1, 1912), 5–8.

9. Diary of Juliet Thompson, National Bahá'í Archives, Wilmette, Ill., entry for Apr. 13, 1912.

10. Ibid., entries for Apr. 15 and Mar. 25, from letter dated Mar. 23, 1912.

11. Dodge, "Abdul-Baha's Arrival in America," p. 5.

12. 'Abdu'l-Bahá, *Promulgation*, pp. 9, 11.

13. "Addresses Delivered by Abdul-Baha in New York City and Vicinity," *Star of the West*, 3, no. 7 (July 13, 1912), 4–5, 10.

14. 'Abdu'l-Bahá, *Promulgation*, p. 22.

15. Ibid., pp. 30–31.
16. Thompson, entry for Apr. 21, 1912.
17. Ibid.
18. 'Abdu'l-Bahá, *Promulgation*, p. 29.

Chapter 3

1. *New York American*, Mar. 1, 1915, p. 16.
2. *Washington Evening Star*, Apr. 21, 1912.
3. Joseph H. Hannen, "Abdul-Baha in Washington, D.C.," *Star of the West*, 3, no. 3 (Apr. 28, 1912), 10.
4. 'Abdu'l-Bahá, *Promulgation*, pp. 36–37.
5. Ibid., p. 41.
6. Ibid., p. 43.
7. Thompson, entry for May 7, 1912.
8. Ibid.
9. 'Abdu'l-Bahá, *Promulgation*, p. 44.
10. Ibid., p. 51.
11. Zia Bagdadi, "'Abdu'l-Bahá in America," *Star of the West*, 19, no. 3 (June 1928), 89.
12. 'Abdu'l-Bahá, *Promulgation*, p. 54.
13. Ibid., p. 57.
14. Bagdadi, "'Abdu'l-Bahá in America," p. 90.
15. *New York American*, Mar. 1, 1915.

Chapter 4

1. 'Abdu'l-Bahá, *Promulgation*, p. 65.
2. Ibid., p. 67.
3. Ibid., pp. 62–63.
4. Bahá'í Houses of Worship, or Temples, are called Mashriqu'l-Adhkárs, an Arabic word meaning the "Dawning Place of the Mention of God." The first one was built in Turkistan, the second in Wilmette, Illinois, where 'Abdu'l-Bahá laid the foundation stone on May 1, 1912. Eventually each city will have a Mashriqu'l-Adhkár.
5. Honore J. Jaxon, "A Stroll with Abdul-Baha," *Star of the West*, 3, no. 4 (May 17, 1912), 29.
6. Ella Goodall and Ella M. Bailey, "Abdul-Baha with the Children of the Friends in Chicago," *Star of the West*, 3, no. 7 (July 13, 1912), 6.
7. 'Abdu'l-Bahá, *Promulgation*, p. 88.

Chapter 5

1. Zia Bagdadi, "'Abdu'l-Bahá in America," *Star of the West*, 19, no. 5

(Aug. 1928), 140–41.
  2. Ibid., p. 141.

Chapter 6

  1. 'Abdu'l-Bahá, *Promulgation*, pp. 107–08.
  2. "Addresses Delivered by Abdul-Baha in New York City and Vicinity," *Star of the West*, 3, no. 7 (July 13, 1912), 12–13.
  3. "Reception to Abdul-Baha by the New York Peace Society at Hotel Astor, May 13, 1912 (Afternoon),"*Star of the West*, 3, no. 8 (Aug. 1, 1912), 13.
  4. Zia Bagdadi, "'Abdu'l-Bahá in America," *Star of the West*, 19, no. 6 (Sept. 1928), 181.
  5. See p. 201 for the text of the article.
  6. Bagdadi, "'Abdu'l-Bahá in America," pp. 181–82.
  7. Ibid., p. 182.
  8. Ibid.
  9. "Addresses Delivered by Abdul-Baha in New York City and Vicinity," *Star of the West*, 3, no. 9 (Aug. 20, 1912), 10.
  10. Ibid., pp. 5–6.
  11. 'Abdu'l-Bahá, *Promulgation*, p. 144.
  12. "Addresses Delivered," *Star of the West*, 3, no. 7 (July 13, 1912), 15.

Chapter 7

  1. "Will Bahaism Unite All Religious Faiths," *The American Review of Reviews*, 45 (June 1912), 748–50.
  2. "The Universal Gospel That Abdul Baha Brings Us," *Current Literature*, 52, no. 6 (June 1912), 676–78.

Chapter 8

  1. 'Abdu'l-Bahá, *Promulgation*, pp. 161, 163–65.
  2. Ibid., pp. 178–79, 181.
  3. Ibid., p. 178.
  4. Ibid., p. 188.
  5. Bahá'u'lláh and 'Abdu'l-Bahá, *Bahá'í World Faith* (Wilmette, Ill.: Bahá'í Publishing Trust, 1956), p. 205.
  6. Abul-Fazl, *The Brilliant Proof* (Chicago: Bahai News Service, 1912).
  7. 'Abdu'l-Bahá, *Promulgation*, p. 201.

Chapter 9

  1. 'Abdu'l-Bahá, *Promulgation*, p. 205.
  2. Ibid., pp. 208–10.

3. Thompson, entry for June 29, 1912.

4. Dr. Ameen U. Fareed, "Barbecue in Honor of Abdul-Baha," *Star of the West*, 3, no. 11 (Sept. 27, 1912), 8.

Chapter 10

1. Hubbard, "A Modern Prophet," pp. 49-51.

2. 'Abdu'l-Bahá, *Promulgation*, p. 213.

3. Thompson, entry for July 5, 1912, about July 4, 1912.

4. "The Persian Prophet" (editorial), *The Independent*, 73 (July 18, 1912), 159–60.

5. Charles Johnston, "A Ray From the East," *Harper's Weekly*, 59 (July 20, 1912), 9.

Chapter 11

1. Joseph H. Hannen, "With Abdul-Baha in Dublin, New Hampshire," *Star of the West*, 3, no. 11 (Sept. 27, 1912), 4.

2. Ibid., pp. 5–6.

Chapter 12

1. Fred Mortensen, "When a Soul Meets the Master," *Star of the West*, 14, no. 12 (Mar. 1924), 366.

2. Ibid., pp. 366–67.

3. The Bahá'í calendar, ordained by the Báb and ratified by Bahá'u'lláh, contains nineteen months of nineteen days each. On the first day of each month, a Feast is held in each Bahá'í community around the world. It consists of three parts—a spiritual portion where the Writings of the Manifestations of God and 'Abdu'l-Bahá are read; a business portion where the Local Spiritual Assembly, the local administrative body, consults with the Bahá'í community; and a social portion, intended to acquaint the Bahá'ís more fully with each other.

Chapter 14

1. Abdul Baha Abbas, "America and World Peace," *The Independent*, 73 (Sept. 12, 1912), 606–09.

Chapter 15

1. "Matrimony in the Bahai Spirit," *Star of the West*, 3, no. 12 (Oct. 16, 1912), 15.

2. Notes of Feny E. Paulson, National Bahá'í Archives, Wilmette, Ill. The house style of the transliteration of Persian and Arabic words has been used.

Chapter 16

1. Mr. Shinji Yamamoto, in a telephone conversation on January 23, 1979, confirmed that his father, Kanichi Yamamoto, arranged the meeting.

2. The Tablet of Visitation is a special prayer honoring the Báb and Bahá'u'lláh; it is read at Their shrines and often used in commemorating Their anniversaries.

Chapter 18

1. 'Abdu'l-Bahá, *Promulgation*, pp. 420–23.

Chapter 19

1. 'Abdu'l-Bahá, *Promulgation*, pp. 448–49.

2. Mohammed Yazdi, "Abdul-Baha in Egypt: A Call to the American Bahais," *Bahai News*, 1, no. 17 (Jan. 19, 1911), 5–7.

3. 'Abdu'l-Bahá, *Promulgation*, p. ii.

4. Irene Earle, "Personals," *The Survey*, 28, no. 4 (Apr. 27, 1912), 179.

5. Notes of William Copeland Dodge, National Bahá'í Archives, Wilmette, Ill.

6. Notes of Lucy Jane Marshall, National Bahá'í Archives, Wilmette, Ill.

7. 'Abdu'l-Bahá, "Training for Service in the Cause of Baha'o'llah," *Star of the West*, 4 (June 24, 1913), 104–05.

8. Notes of Bertha Rohr Clark, National Bahá'í Archives, Wilmette, Ill.

9. Notes of Hazel Tomlinson, National Bahá'í Archives, Wilmette, Ill.

10. 'Abdu'l-Bahá, *Promulgation*, pp. 464, 467.